SMALL MOMENTS, *Sacred Echoes*

Reflections from a Faithful Life

Dr. Janice Brooks

SMALL MOMENTS Sacred Echoes by Dr. Janice Brooks – 2025.

Published by Ash and Resonance Press - 1st Edition - Printed in the United States of America.

ISBN: ISBN: 979-8-9943335-0-1

 The stories expressed in this book are true life stories and happenings from the life of the author as well as those shared with her by others.

Dedication

I dedicate this book to God who gave my life purpose; even when I did not know or understand it. There was a silent strength that carried me for many years and that still small voice that guided me across every bridge, through every valley and every long night. To the Blessed Holy Spirit, I give thanks for every sacred moment that He has divinely directed.

To my daughters I write that you may always know the power of preparation and come to understand the depth of your calling. May you know the God who walks with you through every unknown situation. You are part of the reason I kept moving forward, so that one day you will hopefully understand.

To every reader, please know that this is for you. If you are like me, if you have shed tears and you have cried alone. If you have whispered prayers in silence and held on to that hope that you could not see; to that fire that still burns inside you, please know that this is for you.

God has not forgotten us; He knows that we are not just ordinary, He knows our stories matter because he is God, and He is not finished writing them yet.

Scripture Dedication: (1 Thessalonians 5:24, NIV)
"Faithful is He who calls you, and He also will do it".

About the Author

Dr. Janice Brooks, otherwise known as Dr. Jan, is a woman of faith, perseverance, persistence and deep conviction. Her life has been shaped by life's challenges and refined by God's grace. From a young age she sensed that her life carried a greater purpose and through the difficulties, she has lived out that call with quiet strength and unwavering hope.

Dr. Janice is a Doctor of Ministry (DMin.) and a Christian Counselor and has served in various capacities, as a counselor, teacher of the Word, bank manager and assistant vice president, lecturer, leadership development and strategic life coach, mentor, mother and spiritual encourager. She is always with a heart to uplift others, and with much wisdom gained from real life experiences her voice is honest, reflective and rooted in the Word of God.

This book **Small Moments,** ***Sacred Echoes,*** is born out of years of her personal walk with God, through some ordinary moments that became extraordinary lessons. Her prayer is that each page will help you see your own life through the lens of grace and discover the sacred echoes in your everyday story.

She currently resides in the United States, a native of Jamaica, and continues to invest in the lives of others through coaching, counseling, teaching, writing and quiet acts of service that leave lasting footprints of faith.

SMALL MOMENTS, *Sacred Echoes*

Reflections from a Faithful Life

2025

Sometimes God does not send words, he sends moments in time. He may send wings, a pause, a pattern and even a flicker of beauty in the middle of our stress and silence.

How to Use This Book

This book comes along with your own personal journal. It is written not to be hurried through, but to be received with patience and understanding.

Each chapter is a simple story which is profound, personal and yet universal. These writings are sacred echoes from a faithful life, and they are meant to meet you right where you are.

Here are some ways you may use this devotion to get the best results:

Daily Reading – Set aside a few quiet moments at the beginning of each day to read one chapter, the reflections and prayer. Let it sit with you throughout your day, then read it again if needed at the end of the day.

Journaling Companion – Use the reflective questions or prompts at the end of each chapter to journal and start your own dialogue with God.

Small Group Resource – These chapters can also spark meaningful discussions in group settings or mentoring sessions or coaching relationships. Use it as you see necessary.

Seasonal Encouragement – When you are in a dry, confusing or weary season, you can come back to these pages and let them speak fresh hope into your heart. You may find yourself laughing, crying or even pausing to remember something from your own life and that is the point of this book.

This is not just about my story it is also about what God might want to reveal in yours too for his glory. So go slowly through the pages; go honestly, go with an open heart and most importantly go with God.

Table of Contents

Chapter 1: Chalk Dust and Footprints 6
The unseen impact

Chapter 2: The Echo that Remains 9
Trust God in the waiting

Chapter 3: When the Train Passes 12
Trust God in the waiting

Chapter 4: A Sunday Morning Lesson 17
The need to just be still.

Chapter 5: Top Right Corner 21
Chosen but feel alone in your success.

Chapter 6: Prepared for What I Expected 25
Hope in motion and faith.

Chapter 7: Crossing Over 28
Facing life's bridges with faith, not fear.

Chapter 8: The Weight of Purpose 31
When your calling feels heavier.

Chapter 9: The Power of Through 34
Courage from a place deeper than words.

Chapter 10: The Blessing in the Silence 37
Words may fail but the breath will take over.
Chapter 11: Healing Beyond the Medicine 40
Love is not limited to actions.

Chapter 12: It is going to Rain 43
Miracle waiting in the motion.

Chapter 13: Faith in the start 46
Closing what no longer serves you.

Chapter 14: The Account is Closed 49
Releasing with Grace.

Chapter 15: Put a Word on It 52
The power of simple words.

Chapter 16: Sweep the House 55
When Faith is all you have got to use.

Chapter 17: The Sound of Rain: Pray Again 58
Someone is waiting to hear.

Chapter 18: What Are You Doing Here? 61
Are you where you belong?

Chapter 19: When Are You Going to Obey? 64
God speaks once and twice.

Chapter 20: When Are You Carrying? 67
Not every load is assigned by God.

Chapter 21: The Walk That Changed Everything
When God shows you something new. 70

Chapter 22: Washer Fluid Wisdom 73
A new season with old tactics.

Chapter 23: Too Heavy for the Load 76
Carrying unnecessary burdens.

Chapter 24: The Quiet Strength of Faith 79
Faith does not wear garments of religion.

Chapter 25: The Road to Resilience 83
In the moments where it matters.

Chapter 26: Hidden in Plain Sight 85
Working but watching.

Chapter 27: God had Another Chapter in Mind.
When you don't know, just trust. 88

Chapter 28: The Redefined Assignment.
God had another chapter. 91

Chapter 29: Trust What You See? 94
The clock is ticking.

Chapter 30: Too Good to Be God? 96
Don't move yet.

Chapter 31: When Gratitude Supersedes 99
Do You recognize it?

Chapter 32: Strong but Struggling 102
When strong is weak
Chapter 33: When the Spirit Says Move 105
You see the path no one else sees.

Chapter 34: Waiting for the Ripening
Don't force the fruits. 108

Chapter 35: The Answer You Want
When the answer becomes the truth. 111

Chapter 36: Journey from Knowledge to Truth
Are you a Nicodemus? 114

Chapter 37: When the Wind Changes
Turn back or keep going. 116

Chapter 38: Warmed by the Walk 119
Equipped to walk.

Chapter 39: Unseen Stories, Unexpected Grace
Refuse to ignore. 122

Chapter 40: Teach Me Gently 125
Kindness is a language.

Chapter 41: One Destination Many Faces
Unity in Diversity. 128

Chapter 42: Unity of Our Journey 130
Spiritual history and personal struggles.

Chapter 43: Fruitful and Familiar 132
The quiet blessings.
Chapter 44: The Root of the Matter. 135
Foundation threatened.

Chapter 45: What's Left Behind **138**
Every loss has a lesson.

Chapter 46: When the Strong Hands Grow Still
Not just a neighbor. 140

Chapter 47: Still at the Fence **143**
Love in spite of.

Chapter 48: The Ones Who Didn't Call Back
When the ones go silent. 146

Chapter 49: The Panic, Sigh and Silence
Help me if you can. 149

Chapter 50: When the Hills Remind Me
The power of taking notes. 151

Chapter 51: Sometimes They Are Messengers
They Came as they were sent. 154

Chapter 52: The Dunns River Experience
Discern the time. 157

Chapter 53: God Speaks Through the Leaves
Beckoned to leave. 160

Chapter 54: When the Voice Goes Silent
The presence of peace. 163

Chapter 55: When The Silence Breaks
Returning to the Echoes. 166

Chapter 56: Even The Trees Can Remind Me
Longing for what it was. 169

Chapter 57: The Place Where I Came to Myself
Just in time. 171

Chapter 58: Even The Trees Can Remind You
Take Notice. 173

Chapter 59: Purpose in the Waiting
The Unexpected. 175

Chapter 60: Shelter in the Sudden 178
Comes the awareness.

Chapter 61: After the Rain 180
It does not last forever.

Chapter 62: God Leaves a Pen on the Floor
Provision for purpose. 182

Chapter 63: When God Needs Your Attention
Give without questioning. 185

Chapter 64: The Bell Rings 188
Listening marks time.

Chapter 65: Are We Listening? 190
Only to hear.

Chapter 66: Tending the Soul First 192

Listen to see.

Chapter 67: Ministry of Presence 194
Before you speak.

Chapter 68: Words can Echo 196
From now to Eternity.

Chapter 69 : Seeing the Heart 199
From a place beyond.

Chapter 70: Joy Beyond Circumstances 202
Always at a cost.

Chapter 71: Mountains and Tunnels of Life 205
Past, present and not future.

Chapter 72: The Journey that Spoke 208
When it becomes clear.

Chapter 73: When the Sparrows Came 211
Discern the times.

Chapter 74: The Exit Ramp 214
People will leave so allow them to.

Chapter 75: The Quiet Strength of Faith 217
Unwavering.

Chapter 76: The Enduring Power of a Faith Life 220
A life well lived.

Introduction

We often look for God in big ways, such as in the thunder and in the fire. Yet more often, He speaks in a still small voice; in the everyday moments we sometimes overlook.

This book was born out of my own walk with God, a journey marked not by perfection, but by daily presence. Presence in the classroom, presence on the highway, presence in conversations, detours, delays and even disappointments. Through personal stories, small moments and unexpected reflections, I noticed how God whispers truth, grace and direction into the ordinary moments.

Each entry in this collection is a sacred echo, a moment that stayed with me long after it passed, reminding me that nothing in God is wasted. So, whether you are in a season of clearness or confusion, I pray that these reflections will encourage you to pay attention to your own sacred echoes.

Sometimes the quote on the chalkboard, the car that takes the exit, or the prayer whispered in a long traffic line, carries more weight than we know. May these pages invite you not just to read, but to reflect and most of all to remember that God is in the small moments too.

Walk good and with grace, Dr. Janice.

Sacred Echo: Dedication with love to my mother, Hildred Brooks who left us March 12, 2000. Your legacy lives on in earth and sealed in eternity.

The Quiet Strength of Faith

Psalm 34:18 (NIV)
"The Lord is close to the brokenhearted and saves those who are crushed in spirit."

The heart that gives without counting the cost, the hand that serves without seeking to be recognized, these are the marks of a love that reflects God's own heart.

Part 1: The Selfless Faith of a Mother

There are moments in life when we encounter souls whose quiet acts of love radiate more brightly than any sermon. My mother was one such soul; she did not serve to be seen but she served because she believed God saw it all.

Her life overflowed with a generosity that challenged reason, giving away the last amount of food, sharing the little we had, placing herself in the background so others could move forward. Our home was like a Salvation Army, always a shelter for those who were in need.

She did this not because she had excess, but because she trusted the God who multiplies the little. She lived every day as though His provision was assured. When we lacked anything, her words never changed, it was always "God will provide." He always does as we rarely lacked anything.

Looking back, her life reminds me that faith is not showed when everything is easy, but when everything is scarce and yet we choose to trust God anyway.

You may be in a season like my mother was, giving your best, pouring out what feels like your last drop, trusting God even when you cannot see the outcome. If so, let her example remind you that God sees the sacrifices no one else sees. God honors the faith no one else supports. So, continue to serve with a willing heart, for your quiet obedience is forming a testimony far greater than you know.

Reflection

What areas of your life do you struggle to trust God with, and how can you cultivate a faith that is unshaken by circumstances?

How can you serve others in a way that reflects God's heart of selfless love and trust in His provision?

Prayer

Lord, thank You for the example of my mother who live their life with a quiet, unwavering faith. May I follow in her footsteps, trusting You even when the road is hard, serving others without expecting anything in return, and living in the assurance that You know all things best. I ask that You strengthen my faith, give me a heart of compassion, and remind us that You are near to the brokenhearted. In Jesus' name, Amen.

The Quiet Strength of Faith

Part 2: The Enduring Power of a Faithful Life

1st Thessalonians 3:3 (KJV)
"That no man should be moved by these afflictions: for yourselves know that we are appointed thereunto".

Even when you cannot see the purpose, cling to the truth that God love never leaves you, even in the valley.

My mother lived her life well, always encouraging others and giving her best. Until the day she suffered a stroke, her life changed. She was not the same after that, her body weakened over time, her speech faded and after a while suffering became her constant friend. Yet her faith remained untouched and she never complained, she never murmured and never questioned God. After months of silence, her final words broke through like a divine whisper "God knows all things best."

Those words carry a depth only those who have suffered will truly understand. Her life teaches me that faith does not collapse in hardship it only strengthens, and that God's presence in suffering is not always how we want it, but always near.

You may be in a season like I was, watching someone you love suffer; praying prayers that feel heavy, asking God for mercy or perhaps you are facing a trial that is shaking your soul. If so, take heart because God is near and He is working and God still knows all things best. Even when you cannot see the purpose, cling to the truth that His love never leaves you, even in the valley.

Reflection

What areas of your life do you struggle to trust God with, and how can you practice a deeper surrender?

How can you begin serving others in small, selfless ways that reflect God's heart and your own growing faith?

Prayer

Lord, thank You for the powerful testimonies of those who demonstrate quiet, steadfast faith like my mother did. Help us to trust You in seasons of scarcity, suffering, or uncertainty. Teach us to give generously, love deeply, and follow You with unwavering confidence. Strengthen our heart to believe that You truly know all things best. In Jesus' name, Amen.

Chapter 1

Chalk Dust and Footprints

Galatians 6:9 (KJV)
"And let us not be weary in well doing: for in due season, we shall reap, if we faint not".

Sometimes the smallest act of your presence leaves the deepest imprints on the soul of others. You may speak for a moment but the echo lives on in eternity.

Some years ago, I had the opportunity to lecture at a well-known university in their evening program. Even though financial management was not my strongest subject in college, I was blessed to teach four finance courses.

The students were not what you would expect in a typical university classroom. There were no fresh-faced teenagers eager to explore the financial world; instead, there were only experienced people: mothers, fathers, office workers, stay home moms and even some dreamers who all worked by day and studied by night.

At first when I was asked, I did not think much about the opportunity beyond teaching the course outline. I had no big plans to change any lives or share any life-changing wisdom. Yet something shifted in me during that first week of class; something told me I was there for more than teaching. Maybe it was the weariness I saw in their eyes or at times the quiet hunger that spoke louder than the questions they asked. Without any hesitation, I started writing a quote on the blackboard before each class.

Sometimes I used scripture and at other times I wrote my own thoughts or quotes from poets and philosophers, whatever inspired me that day. Then we would sit in open discussion for about ten minutes, just talking. There were no pressure and each person shared as they felt led to. There was just the sound of our hearts connecting in a sacred space of shared encouragement.

Over time those ten minutes became almost like a ritual for the class and for me too. Each evening a hush would fall over the class, and you could almost feel the burdens lifted from their shoulders just long enough for them to breathe, hope and believe again.

Stay tuned for part two in the next chapter where something unexpected happened that reminded me and maybe you too how the smallest doings can have the biggest impact.

Reflection

In what ways can your actions, whether big or small, positively influence the lives of others and why is it important to be aware of this impact?

How does making a positive impact on others contribute to your own personal growth?

Prayer

Dear Father, please entrust to me souls who will reflect your glory. Let those You place in my care be shaped by your truth, strengthened by our Spirit, and drawn ever closer to your heart. May my life be a vessel through which your light shines and may the echo of your glory resound through generations. In Jesus' name, Amen.

Chapter 2

The Echo that Remains

Hebrews 6:10 (KJV)
"For God *is* not unrighteous to forget your work and labor of love, which ye have shewed toward his name, in that ye have ministered to the saints, and do minister".

Sometimes you speak only once but your words keep walking with someone for the rest of their life journey.

One day I was late because I got caught in traffic while heading to class. Lost in my own thoughts, I rushed into the classroom and overlooked the chalkboard, I skipped the talk and dived right into the lesson. Halfway through a sentence about an economic principle, I heard a voice from the back of the class. "Miss," the student said gently, "why didn't we start with the quote today?"

I was surprised by the question, but before I could answer another student said, "Yes Miss, the quote and the talk. They set the tone every evening and make the class lighter." Then another student spoke up, "It is the only quiet space I have all week where I feel like I can breathe again."

In that moment it felt like the classroom had become a sanctuary. I wanted to cry and not stop crying. The chalkboard which was just a place to write on during the lectures, had become a place for the many hearts in front of me. The quotes which were sometimes written in haste and inspired by the Holy Spirit, were unknowing to me messages for all of us. The discussions though sometimes brief as they were, had become a lifeline for many of those students.

Yet had I known, maybe I would have done differently? Or would I really? I don't know. Think about it, is that not the quality of our spiritual service?

The real kind when we give to others without expecting anything in return, when we offer help and comfort without counting the cost.

At times we do not see or understand the seeds we plant daily, but God sees and sometimes we get small glimpses, moments like these when the veil is lifted and we get to witness the harvest.

That night I cried on my way home and continued to cry when I got home. It was not out of sorrow but from gratitude. Everything that happened that evening reminded me that purpose often shows up quietly without any fuss and the footprints we leave in the spirit are not always seen with the natural eye, but they echo through eternity.

Since that day, I never missed the quote, not even once. Even when the semester ended and the students went in different directions like leaves in the wind; I felt and knew something sacred had happened in that classroom. The blackboard was wiped clean each night, but the words were already written not with the chalk but in the hearts of many.

Reflection

Make your own notes as to how this story has impacted your life and maybe you recall one of your own.

What has God entrusted you with and how are you taking care of that assignment?

Pray that God will place souls into your care that will echo his glory.

Prayer

Thank you, Dear God, for reminding us that sometimes the smallest acts of our presence can leave the deepest marks on the souls of others. We may speak for a moment, but the echo lives on forever into eternity. In Jesus' name Amen.

Chapter 3

When the Train Passes

Isaiah 40:31 (KJV)
"But they that wait upon the Lord shall renew their strength; they shall mount up with wings as eagles; they shall run and not be weary; and they shall walk and not faint".

Trust God in the waiting because He sees ahead and he knows your train will move again.

My friend Claudine shared with me this powerful story that ministered to me in a sobering way, and I rewrote it to share with you so that it may bless you too.

The noise of the train had long gone, and the place had an uneasy silence. Claudine said that she sat almost motionless beneath the dim lights of the subway car with her hands resting in her lap and her thoughts in turmoil. Her thoughts were racing, "why did this happen?" She had just finished another difficult day at the office, and her spirit was worn like the hem of a worn coat. The train which was the one thing she counted on to take her home had come to a dead stop on the tracks.

She said outside the thick windows of the train was an eerie stillness that almost whispered back as if to say there was no one going and no one coming. Then suddenly she heard a jumbled announcement that came through the speakers "Delay due to obstruction on the tracks"; That was it and nothing more was said.

Some time passed and Claudine looked at her watch and then glanced around. Many of the passengers shifted in their seats, sighing and checking their phones that seemed to have little or no signal. An older man who was standing near the door muttered a prayer under his breath. A little boy clutched his mother's coat with his eyes full of questions. The train was still and with it so was the rest of life inside the train.

Many minutes had passed, and they turned half an hour, and the time kept moving but the train was not moving. Then more time passed and Claudine's anxiety began to grow. She had somewhere to go and she should be moving, getting further along. Waiting in those moments felt like a kind of death to her, a type of surrender to something invisible and oppressive.

Claudine said the longer she sat there, the louder her inner voice spoke: "You must do something, you cannot just stay here as nothing is going to change unless you move." So, against the tug of heart she stood up, gripped the pole beside her seat, and walked straight to the door. The emergency exit was unlocked and a few others stepped forward too while others watched but said nothing.

Claudine stepped onto the narrow ledge of the track walkway, her shoes sounding on the floor, her heart racing and her mind told her she was doing the right thing. It may have been the same for the few others who were also taking action. After all she said, any form of progress was better than sitting still, which is what she thought.

She walked along quickly with each footstep echoing into a question she could not answer. It was less than five minutes outside that she heard the train coming, the deep rumbling sound like a judgement sound behind her.

The train she had left behind was moving, coming her way. The lights shone in the dark more like a revelation. She stepped aside into the safety alcove and so did the few others, while they watched as the train passed by, car after car, window after window, seat after seat. Claudine said she saw the place she had sat, it was empty now and the train was moving but she was not on it.

As I thought about her story, I believe this is life in a spiritual sense too. At times we find ourselves waiting in uncomfortable silence, stillness with nothing happening. There are even seasons when it feels like life has stopped, like God has gone quiet and like every prayers are echoing back void. In our restlessness and impatience, we tell ourselves that delay may mean denial. We think maybe we should do something or just take control of the situation.

Look at it this way, if my friend Claudine had stayed just a little longer, she would have been on the train getting home on time. In her uneasiness, she missed what was her miracle; not because the miracle did not come, but because she did not wait long enough to receive it.

Remember this "But those who trust in the LORD will find new strength. They will soar high on wings like eagles. They will run and not grow weary. They will walk and not faint". (Isaiah 40:31, NLT). Faith does not always look like movement, sometimes trusting God looks like staying in place and not moving. Trust God in the waiting, because he is God and he sees ahead and he knows your train will move again.

Reflection

The train always moves again, but the question is, will we still be on it when it does?

Make your own notes as to how this story has impacted your life and maybe you recall one of your own. Pray that God will give you wisdom to wait.

Prayer

Dear father, please help me to trust you in the waiting. Sometimes it is not easy Lord, and it carries a lot of weight. Yet in those moments remind me that faith is not equal to movement, sometimes it is about resting in you as the steps of a righteous man is ordered by God and you know the plans you have for my life in Jesus' name Amen.

Chapter 4

A Sunday Morning Lesson

Exodus 14:14 (KJV)
"The Lord will fight for you; you need only to be still".

Our role is not always to strive but sometimes to be still and trust God.

It was just past 5:15 AM. on a quiet Sunday morning; I was on an early morning errand. The streets were silent and the place felt like the world was just waking up. I sat alone in my car parked with the atmosphere inside and out was peaceful. While I waited, I turned on the radio to listen to the calm and comfort of an early morning Christian service. Those sacred hours when it felt like heaven seemed just a bit closer.

At exactly 5:30 a.m. I felt like something was shifting, the music stopped and the radio went silent. Suddenly it felt as if there was stillness in the car more like a mystery. I looked up very puzzled because I did not turn the radio off. Just them the dashboard light came on with a quiet but powerful message: "System turned off to preserve your battery."

Wow! That was all I could say, and in that small digital moment, I heard something more than just the manufacturer logic, I heard God.

Think about this, so many of us live like that with our human engines off but our systems are still running. We sit still but we are losing power; we are sleeping but we are not resting, we may be listening, but we are not hearing anything that is being said.

Just like my vehicle, sometimes God need to get some words to us, like, "I have turned this off for you to preserve your power."

We sometimes think life means constantly doing things, always being "on", however a spiritual Christ-centered person knows the value of preserving, of stillness and of silent obedience. Sometimes the most powerful thing we can ever do is nothing at all. It is not being lazy, and it is not avoiding our duties, but it is just intentional stillness. I like to call it a time of holy waiting.

The same way that my car turned off to conserve what little battery it had, the Holy Spirit sometimes powers us down to protect our inner man, because a drained life is a dangerous one, not just to others, but to ourselves.

Remember this, preservation is not punishment it is preparation. Even Jesus withdrew himself for a while so that he could prepare. He slept in the storms; he turned away from the crowds to talk with his Father. He did these to protect his power so He could give it fully when it was time.

So maybe that morning was not just a digital moment for me to be aware of; maybe it was a divine reminder that God was whispering to me to be still, probably saying "Let Me sustain you, just turn off the systems and listen not to the radio, but to Me."

So, to every leader, every servant, every believer and every person feeling the drain, please do not ignore the signs. Do not hate the silence or fight the off switch; because when God turns something off, He is not making an end of it, He is only preserving it.

The next time you power back on you will be stronger and more ready. Let every silent moment teach you to be still and allow the Holy Spirit to lead you. Be still because God is fighting for you. Wait on Him because your strength is being preserved and renewed.

Reflection

Remember just like a car shutting down to preserve battery, God sometimes silences our activity to remind us: He is the source of strength, and our role is not always to strive, but sometimes to be still and trust.

In what area of your life do you need to turn the switch off to preserve your relationship with God?

Make your own notes as to how this story has impacted your life and maybe you recall one of your own. Pray that God will give you faith to trust him more.

Prayer

Dear God, I am guilty of constant movement, always having the switch on. Help me today to power off so I can hear from you because you do not shout above the noise, you speak in the quiet movements. Help me Father in Jesus name Amen.

Chapter 5

Top Right Corner

Romans 12:6 (NLT)
"In his grace, God has given us different gifts for doing certain things well. So, if God has given you the ability to prophesy, speak out with as much faith as God has given you".

Your name does not need to be first or loud or famous. It just needs to be found where God placed it. Destiny is not about placement; it is about purpose.

We were all created to be the best; and I have always believed that. It is not in the sense of outperforming others, but in fulfilling the highest version of what God planned for each of us.

I learned this early, even though I did not fully understand it at the time. I was in fifth grade when I sat the Common Entrance Exam to qualify for high school. Thirteen of us from my class took it together, wide-eyed, hopeful, bonded by shared dreams and sharpened pencils.

The results took nearly three months to be published, and we waited through hot days and sleepless nights, wondering if our names would appear among the thousands, then finally the newspaper came.

I can still feel the crispness of the pages, the black ink glistering as we turned, page by page, scanning rows of tiny names. Then out of nowhere, there was my name. Perched in the top right-hand corner of the second to last page. A flood of emotion hit me all at once; I jumped, I shouted and I cried.

Yet even as my heart soared in gladness, it broke for the others and so we continued searching, my teacher Miss Brown and me. Then finally we gave up as we could not find the names of my other twelve classmates. Joy and sorrow sat in the same space that day. I celebrated but I also mourned it because I was chosen but they were not, or at least, that is how it felt.

Years later, I see the lesson hidden in that moment because sometimes your call will separate you and sometimes being set apart feels a lot like being set aside. *E*ven when you are the one who "made it". You will grow to realize that God's calling is not about comparison, it is about assignments.

Later in life I learned that elevation is not just about success, it is about stewardship. When you are called higher, you are also called to carry more; to lead, serve and to stay humble.

I also learned not to mistake the absence of someone else's name next to mine as failure. Their path might be different, slower, or written in a different paper altogether. God's timing is never confined to a single publication date.

We were all created to be the best, just not all at the same time, in the same way, or on the same page. Each of us is wired uniquely, called specifically and measured not by rankings or roles, but by faithfulness to our divine design.

Reflection

Your name does not need to be first, loud or famous. It just needs to be found where God placed it. Destiny is not about placement. It is about purpose.

Think of a time when you received something that set toy apart from others, how did you feel and what did you do?

Make your own notes as to how this story has impacted your life and maybe you recall one of your own. Pray that God will give you faith to trust him more.

Prayer

Dear God, thank you that you are the giver of all good things. Help me to be thankful for all blessings big or small, not just for myself but for others. Let me understand that each person is made special in your sight and you may lift one up and put down another not because of their standing, but for your glory in Jesus name.

Chapter 6

Prepared for What I Expected

Romans 5:3–5 (NIV)
"Not only so, but we also glory in our sufferings, because we know that suffering produces perseverance; perseverance, character; and character, hope. And hope does not put us to shame, because God's love has been poured out into our hearts through the Holy Spirit, who has been given to us".

Hope is not a wish, but it is preparation in motion, sacrifice fueled by expectation and grounded in faith.

Hope is not wishful thinking, it is the deep, quiet conviction that what you are working toward, praying over, sacrificing for and crying through will one day bear fruit.

For a long time I lived with that conviction. I had two jobs, one my official title, the other what some would call a side hustle. Ironically, the side hustle brought in more money and required more of me. My goal was simple, and huge, it was to buy a home, pay university tuition for myself and ensure both my daughters completed high school with every opportunity possible.

I wanted more for myself and also for them; I wanted stability and so I prepared for what I wanted and expected. That meant long days and even longer nights traveling across countries, walking from store to store for sixteen hours, sometimes on a Sunday, often in places that were not well known. Then catching a flight early Monday morning just to be back in time for my "main" job.

There was not enough time to go home, to get rested or dressed; so I would change clothes at the airport or in my car, drive at top legal speed and show up at work with a fresh face and professional look. My coworkers never knew the miles I traveled, the weight I carried or even the faith that fueled me but I knew and God knew.

I did not always see the results in those moments, but I kept moving, kept working and hoping. There were times when hope whispered to me when no one else did, as if to say, keep going, this will all be worth it.

Now I look back and I see what it was, I see the houses, the degrees, I see my daughters walking through the very doors I prayed would open for them. Now I know that hope is not inactive, it is prophetic at times, it prepares us and it invests in a future it cannot yet see but believes will come.

Reflection

What are you preparing for today that no one else sees?

Can you trust that God sees it and will honor it in His time?

Prayer

Lord, help me stay faithful in the unseen seasons. Strengthen my hope when I am weary and remind me that You are the rewarder of those who diligently seek You. Help me to seek you because you are a present help in Jesus name Amen.

Chapter 7

Crossing Over

Isaiah 43:2 (NLT)
"When you go through deep waters, I will be with you. When you go through rivers of difficulty, you will not drown. When you walk through the fire of oppression, you will not be burned up; the flames will not consume you".

Bridges teach us what fear forgets: the only way over is through and the only direction is forward.

In all way bridges are built for a purpose; they are everywhere and are an unavoidable feature in almost every country, city and town. Some are short and easy to cross while others stretch for miles over deep waters, connecting places that would otherwise remain divided.

Driving from one state to another is never simple, especially if it is your first time on the route and there is usually some level of uncertainty in the unknown. There is also hesitation and if you are anything like me, there is also a healthy dose of inner self talk especially when there is a bridge involved.

You see, I have never been fond of crossing bridges, and whenever I plan a long road trip, I check the route not just for traffic but for bridges. Particularly the high ones those that cross over water, the same ones that make your palms sweat before you even start the engine.

There was one trip in particular where I convinced myself, "You can do this because You are bold," but the truth was, I was not entirely sure and as I approached the bridge my thoughts raced. What if I panic? What if I stop? What if I cannot make it?

Then the reminder came, bridges are made to cross over so you cannot stop halfway. There are no exits and no turnarounds; once you are on, you have no choice but to keep moving forward.

That is the part I have grown to love most, not the design, not the height, not the view but the challenge they offer. Isn't that the same with life? Life is a lot like a bridge; it will bring you to places where fear wants to paralyze you, where uncertainty whispers that it is safer to go back; but turning around is not an option because God does not lead us backward, He leads us through.

Whether you are in a season of transition, a major decision, or a personal trial, your bridge moment will come. In that moment you must decide, will I move forward in faith even when I do not feel brave?

Crossing over is not about never feeling fear, it is about not letting fear drive you to go back. It is about trusting that if God brought you to the bridge, He would take you across it; then on the other side you will look back with your heart racing, hands even trembling and shout or whisper, "I did it, with God, I did it."

Reflection

Is there a "bridge" in your life right now that you are hesitant to cross?

What would moving forward look like, even one step at a time?

Prayer

Lord, help me to trust You when I reach the bridges in life. Give me courage when I feel afraid and remind me that forward is the only direction You have called me to walk. In Jesus name Amen

Chapter 8

The Weight of Purpose

2 Corinthians 4:17 (NIV)
"For our light and momentary troubles are achieving for us an eternal glory that far outweighs them all".

Even when the journey is heavy, it produces something glorious in you, something greater than the weight you feel today.

The first time I went to a bowling alley, I was surprised by the weight of the balls. Watching bowling on television, it all looked so smooth and even effortless. Players made it seem like the balls glide from their hands, light as air. Then the moment I lifted one for myself, I realized these things were heavy and I had misjudged their weight significantly.

That is how it is with purpose? We watch others live out their calling and assume it must be easy. From a distance, it looks smooth, graceful and polished; but when it is your turn to carry what you were born to carry, you suddenly realize, this has weight and real weight too.

The weight of purpose is not decided by appearance, but it is decided by the one who designed it, and the one who dares to carry it.

From the age of thirteen, I knew there was something more to my life. I could not explain it but I felt it, a pull, a whisper, a deep awareness that my life had meaning beyond what I could see. But I did not know then how much that purpose would cost. I did not know the strength it would demand and the courage it would require, more so the weight it would carry.

Later in life, I would walk through painful seasons of abuse, attacks and disappointments; even setbacks that would make most people fold. Yet still I kept moving, not because I was strong, but because I had no choice; my purpose was heavy but it was also holy.

Over time, I realized that weight is not a punishment, it is a measurement that shows you that your life has depth; that your assignment is not common and that the refining of your character is part of the preparation for your calling.

Purpose will not always be light and it will not always feel manageable, but it will always be worth it. Then I learn that what God designs he also strengthens and what He places on your life, He also equips you to carry and finish.

Remember that *t*he weight of your purpose is not a burden; it is evidence that your life carries eternal value and if it feels heavy, it is because it matters.

Reflection

Have you miscalculated the weight of your own calling?

What parts of your journey have proven just how strong God is within you?

Prayer

Father, help me not to run from the weight of my purpose. Teach me to carry it with grace, to trust Your strength in my weakness, and to remember that heaviness is not a sign of failure but of calling. In Jesus name Amen.

Chapter 9

The Power of Through

Isaiah 43:2 (KJV)
"When thou passest through the waters, I will be with thee; and through the rivers, they shall not overflow thee: when thou walkest through the fire, thou shalt not be burned; neither shall the flame kindle upon thee".

Strength is not found in avoiding the journey, but in enduring it with God.

Are you fascinated by long tunnels, huge forests, and high mountains? Well, I was at a point in my life because they have such vastness and at times, if you venture in, the only way out of them is to go through.

Our childhood home was settled in the rural countryside, surrounded by wooded lands, wide grassy fields, treacherous hillsides and deep slopes. We learned to maneuver our way through them daily on our journey to and from school as there were no other routes or shortcuts. The only way was to go through the hills and that was when I first understood the power of "through."

As children we learned to walk with purpose and intention, usually armed with knowledge of our terrain; we were always prepared for the journey. We knew the steep drops, the soft patches of earth that could give way under our feet, and the spots where the sun peeked through the canopy just enough to offer hope. We were never surprised as we were trained by the path.

In life just as in childhood, there are terrains we must travel in the form of painful seasons, uncertainty, waiting and even loss. These are not places we can bypass as there are no detours around grief, no shortcuts through growth, and no skipping the valleys that lead to the mountains. Like it was back then on our countryside journey, the only way is still through.

You may be going through something now or it may come up later, it may be a deep valley or a long uphill climb. Remember that the goal is not just in surviving it, but in knowing who is walking with you. The terrain may be tough, but the journey is holy and most important, the only way may be through, but you are not going alone.

The God we serve does not always pluck us out of hard places. Instead, He promises His presence as we pass through them. He does not say, "If," he says "When" implying a level of certainty in our trials. Yet with that certainty comes an even greater promise: we will not be alone because His presence sustains, strengthens, and secures us.

Reflection

What memory of the trails in your youth or other times gave you confidence?

What situations have you endured where the presence of God was your peace?

Prayer

Father, Thank You for being the God who walks with us through every season. When the way is dark, remind us of Your light. When the path is steep, give us strength for each step. Teach us to trust Your presence more than we fear the journey. And may we always remember that "through" with You is better than "around" without You. In Jesus' name, Amen.

Chapter 10

The Blessing in the Silence

Romans 8:26 (NIV)
"In the same way, the Spirit helps us in our weakness. We do not know what we ought to pray for, but the Spirit himself intercedes for us through wordless groans".

When words fail, let your breath become your prayer and God hears it all.

I can still remember the time when it seemed that everything I had hoped for, prayed for and fasted for finally arrived. The moment felt like a long-awaited answer, wrapped in favor and promise. I was convinced this was it, that this was the blessing. Yet less than two years later everything began to unravel.

What once looked like destiny began to crumble and what felt like fulfillment started to feel like betrayal. Was this not an answered prayer? Did not the mother of the church say, "God says? and did not I believe it with all my heart?

Then the pain, disappointment, failure and what felt like loss in the moment came in like a flood and with them, silence. I could no longer find the words, not to pray, not to explain and not even to scream; there was just silence. I did not want to quote Scriptures or sing worship songs, I just wanted to breathe, because breathing was all I had left.

Sometimes that is enough because I remember in the Bible, Jacob found himself in a midnight wrestling match with the angel of the Lord. He had reached a breaking point in his life, confronting fear, his past and the uncertainty of his future. The Scripture in Genesis chapter 32 tells us he wrestled all night until the break of day. So tough was the struggle that his hip was dislocated, leaving him with a permanent limp; but Jacob refused to let go until he received a blessing.

I believe he did not have the right words, nor did he have perfect faith, instead he had pain and he had a grip of the angel who carried the blessings. Sometimes that is what endurance looks like; just holding on when words will not come and understanding is out of reach. When your prayers become groans and your songs become sighs.

There will be moments when you have nothing left but breath, no eloquent prayers and no emotional strength, but just your breath. Yet in those moments, God leans in closer and He hears the language of our silence. He understands the tears we do not cry and the pain we cannot explain.

So when words refuse to show up just breathe and know that the breath is your proof you are still here; still holding on and that God is still working, even in the silence. He says, just breathe, because your life is in every breath. "Then the LORD God formed a man from the dust of the ground and breathed into his nostrils the breath of life, and the man became a living being". (Genesis 2:7, NIV)

Reflection

Like Jacob, sometimes you will not walk away from struggle the same, but you will walk away changed. Maybe even with a limp but also with a blessing.

What are you holding onto today that feels like a fight in the dark?

Have you allowed yourself the grace to simply breathe when the words will not come?

Prayer

Lord in my struggle, stay with me. When fear rises and the night feels long, give me the courage to hold on to You. Do not let my trial end without Your blessing. Rename what is broken in me, strengthen what is weak, and let this wrestle become my transformation. In Jesus name Amen.

Chapter 11

Healing Beyond Medicine

John 4:18 (NIV)
"There is no fear in love. But perfect love drives out fear, because fear has to do with punishment. The one who fears is not made perfect in love".

When truth finally meets the places we hide, it doesn't shame us it frees us to be known and in being known, we are being healed.

The doctor's office was never my favorite place as a child. For me and my siblings and even the other kids in our neighborhood, the mere thought of a visit sparked dread in our minds. Not because we did not trust the doctors, but because we feared what the visit might require bitter medicines, cold instruments or worse an injection. There were times we would hide our symptoms hoping to avoid the trip altogether.

Yet somehow, something strange always happens because the moment we walked through the clinic doors, the fear began to fade. We would laugh nervously in the waiting area, eyeing the candy jar with hope that it would still be there when we got in. Those little "fear-relieving candies" felt like a sacred reward. It was as if the doctor knew just how to reach into a child's heart and say, "You are safe now."

What amazed me most, looking back, is how often we would begin to feel better before we were even seen by the doctor. Just being there, in that place of healing even with all our fear, was sometimes enough to begin our recovery.

I think our walk with God is a bit like that. There are seasons when we are afraid to come to Him, afraid of what He will say, what He might change, or how much it might hurt to be honest. We carry our spiritual illnesses and emotional wounds in silence, pretending everything is fine, when we are really not doing well. Yet just like with those childhood doctor visits, healing often begins the moment we choose to step into His presence.

God does not always prescribe quick fixes or give us sugar-coated solutions, but He does offer love that drives out fear. Sometimes He even gives us small signs, ones we could name "divine candies." These may be tiny moments of peace, comfort or unexpected joy that remind us we are loved, seen and safe with Him.

Reflection

Is there an area of your life where your life you been avoiding God out of fear of what He might reveal or require?

How have you experienced His "fear-relieving love" in moments of vulnerability or weakness?

Prayer

Heavenly Father, Thank You for being the Great Physician of my heart. You know my fears even before I speak to them, and You meet me with gentleness and love. Help me to come to You honestly and often, knowing that You are not a place of punishment, but of peace. Heal what I am afraid to face, and remind me daily that in Your presence, I am safe and I am loved in In Jesus' name, Amen.

Chapter 12

It is Going to Rain

Matthew 5:45 (NIV)
"That you may be children of your Father in heaven. He causes his sun to rise on the evil and the good and sends rain on the righteous and the unrighteous".

God's love is not limited by our actions; it shines on the righteous and the unrighteous alike.

It is going to rain today!" That is the meteorologist's familiar declaration that stirs different emotions in different people. For some, it is cause for celebration, especially after a long, dry stretch of heat. For others, particularly in areas where rainfall is constant or unpredictable, it may be met with weariness or dread.

When I lived in a small farming community in the deep countryside of Jamaica, rain was more than a weather report, it was a lifeline. Most families depended on the land for their survival, and the rainy season meant watered crops, full barrels and hope for the future.

I had a love-hate relationship with the rain. I loved the smell of the earth as the first drops hit dry ground and I loved the way the community seemed to come alive, farmers rejoicing, children playing barefoot in puddles. I also remember the times when the rain would not stop, when it poured so heavily that the ground gave way and crops washed out, paths eroded and Joy gave way to anxiety.

Think about it, is not that so much like life? We pray for blessings and when they come, we rejoice. Yet sometimes the very things we asked for come in an unexpected volume. The relationship we prayed for becomes demanding; the opportunity we dream of brings stress and the season of growth sometimes includes loss. So just like the rain, God's blessings can come with both refreshment and personal responsibility.

Yet even when the rain is too much, even when it seems to erode rather than nourish, God is still present. The same rain that causes flooding today may feed the harvest tomorrow. The same rain that makes roads impassable may refill the rivers that sustain life.

The rain reminds us of God's sovereignty, how He gives and takes, how He waters our lives in both ways we understand and ways we do not understand and even in the sorrow of what was lost, there is still reason to store up hope for what He will bring.

Reflection

Have there been "rainy seasons" in your life that felt more like erosion than blessing? Looking back, how did God meet you in that time?

How can you store up spiritual strength in your dry seasons, so that you are prepared when the rain comes?

Prayer:

Lord, Thank You for the rain, both the kind that waters the earth and the kind that grows my soul. Help me to trust You in every season, whether I feel refreshed or worn down. Remind me that even when things feel washed away, you are working for my good. Teach me to store up wisdom, peace, and faith so that I can withstand life's storms and receive Your blessings with open hands and a ready heart. In Jesus' name, Amen.

Chapter 13

Faith in the Start

2 Corinthians 5:7 (NIV)
"For we walk by faith, not by sight".

God often reveals provision not at the beginning of the journey, but in the steps, we dare to take by faith.

There are moments in life when everything in the natural world tells us to sit still, to wait until we see resources, or certainty but sometimes God asks us to move in faith before we see the answer.

One morning, I found myself with no food, no money and an empty gas tank. I had a job, a car and more than a mustard seed of determination and faith. I had no one to call for help, but I did have a belief that if I started, God would somehow meet me along the way.

So I got ready and got in my car; the gas light was glowing red, warning me that I did not have enough to get anywhere. Still, I said aloud, "Lord, please do not let this car run out of gas on the road. Please help me to get to work." I started out and kept driving and I had no intention of looking down at the gas gauge in the dashboard, after all faith is not about what you see.

Travelling from Portmore to Manor Park, for those who know the distance, was not a quick fifteen-minute journey. Halfway through the drive, I looked down and saw something that stunned me. The red gas warning light was gone and the fuel gauge, which had been flat on empty, now read a little above empty tank. I was nearly speechless, overwhelmed by the reality that something miraculous had happened.

I kept driving and kept praying and I made it to work. By the end of the day, God had provided the money I needed to fill my tank and get back home. The provision came, but only after I decided to move. I am convinced the car was not malfunctioning, it was God responding to faith in motion.

What if I had not started the engine? What if I had let fear and lack stop me from trying? I would have missed a divine moment which is the proof that faith, no matter how small, moves the heart of God.

You too may be wondering if you should start and if you should step out when you feel empty, unsure, or unqualified? Remember this: faith does not wait for signs of fullness. Faith moves even when the tank reads empty as the miracle might just be waiting in your movement.

Reflection

What area of your life is God calling you to move in faith even when you cannot see the full provision?

Have you ever delayed action because you were waiting for all the resources to appear first?

Prayer

Heavenly Father, thank You for being my Provider even when I cannot see the way. Help me to trust You enough to move forward when everything in me wants to wait. Increase my faith, even if it is just a little, and remind me that You meet me in my steps not just at my destination. In Jesus' name, Amen.

Chapter 14

The Account is Closed

Psalm 90:12 (NIV)
"Teach us to number our days, that we may gain a heart of wisdom".

When the account is closed, the balance does not lie in what we have done, but in what grace has already paid. Our debt was settled long before we ever knew.

In the banking world, closing an account is a regular task. It is rarely dramatic matter but more often a procedural one, yet it is always intentional. Whether due to a customer relocation, dissatisfaction, or shifting needs, there is always a reason behind the decision.

I have watched bank employees handle these closures with quiet authority. Yet, even in such a routine task, for me there is always a subtle moment sometimes marked by empathy or reflection. What did this account mean once to the person? What brought them to this decision? Behind every number is a story, a season and perhaps a sacrifice.

It made me think that in our spiritual and emotional lives, we too carry accounts. Openings and closings of chapters, relationships, dreams, habits and commitments. Some we manage well, others we allow to stay open far too long, accumulating emotional overdrafts and spiritual debt.

Just like in banking, there comes a time when we must evaluate: Is this relationship still bearing fruit? Is this commitment aligned with God's purpose? Is this habit drawing me closer to Christ or further from peace?

There is no shame in closing what no longer serves your growth in God. In Matthew chapter 10 and verse 14, Jesus Himself told His disciples to shake the dust off their feet when a town refused to receive them, that too was a kind of account closure.

Now here is the key, just as a banker closes an account with records, reflection and sometimes a final statement, we too must close our spiritual accounts with prayer, wisdom, and grace. Some doors are not slammed shut they are gently closed, honored for what they once were and surrendered back to God.

Reflection

Are there any "accounts" in your life: relationships, commitments, or mindsets that God may be asking you to evaluate or close?

What would it look like for you to release something with grace, rather than guilt?

Prayer

Father God, Thank You for the seasons You have allowed me to walk through, and for the people and places that have shaped my journey. Give me discernment to know when something no longer aligns with Your purpose for my life. Help me to close doors with peace, not bitterness; with gratitude, not regret. I trust you to lead me into what is next with wisdom and grace. In Jesus' name, Amen.

Chapter 15

Put a Word on It

Proverbs 18:21 (KJV)
"Death and life are in the power of the tongue: and they that love it shall eat the fruit thereof".

Your words shape your world and what you dare to speak in faith today can become reality tomorrow.

Years ago, I longed to create a better life for myself and my children. One of the biggest dreams I had was owning a home, but it felt out of reach, almost unrealistic. In the front of my mind, I kept hearing voices of doubt: "This is not for you, you cannot afford it and no one in your family has ever done this, why do you think you can?

Yet somehow, somewhere deep inside another phrase kept quietly rising: "Put a word on it." I did not even fully understand what those words meant at the time, but something in my spirit stirred and I began driving through a neighborhood that felt like a dream.

There were clean streets, well-kept homes and a sense of peace in the atmosphere. It was not on my way to anywhere, but I had to go out of my way just to see it, and I kept going.

Even with nothing tangible in hand, I would stretch my hand toward the houses and speak aloud: "This is where I want to live. I am going to buy a house here." Little did I know, I was putting a word on it. I planted a seed with my faith and watered it every time I spoke life into that dream.

Months later, while scanning the local newspaper, I saw a home listed in that very neighborhood. I called the owner and set up a visit. I had no funds at the time, but I had faith. By God's grace, the owner reduced the price by over twenty percent and doors opened that only He could have opened.

Today, I still own that home, a dream that once felt impossible became my reality; all because I spoke it in faith before I saw it in fullness. I did not understand everything at the time, but I now know the power that rests in speaking God's promises over our lives, even when the circumstances say otherwise.

You too may be questioning your dreams, wondering if you are crazy for believing something so far beyond your current means. What if the breakthrough starts not with a bank account or a perfect plan, but with your voice? Now start speaking it and declaring it and put a word on it and watch what God will do.

Reflection

Is there a dream or promise you have been afraid to speak out loud because it feels too big or too far away?

What are some life-giving words you can begin declaring over your future today?

Prayer

Lord, help me to speak words of faith even when fear and doubt try to silence me. Let the words of my mouth align with the dreams You have planted in my heart. Give me courage to declare Your promises and believe that nothing is impossible with You. In Jesus' name, Amen.

Chapter 16

Sweep the House

Isaiah 52:12 (NIV)
"But you will not go out in a hurry. You will not leave as if you were running for your lives. For the Lord will go before you. And the God of Israel will keep watch behind you".

When God commands a sweep, it is never just about the broom, it is about removing what no longer honors your prayers, your peace or your purpose.

For years, I was treated with disregard by the very ones closest to me. The kind of pain I carried was not visible, not bruises or broken bones, but wounds that pierced the heart. Their actions coupled with careless words and emotional neglect seemed weightless to them, but to me they were soul-crushing.

I prayed often desperately for God to deliver me and I wanted Him to intervene in clean and ordinary ways such as a conversation, a turning of hearts or even a gentle resolution. Yet God does not always work the way we expect.

One day, I heard God say, "Sweep the house." It seemed odd, even ordinary because I usually sweep my house every day. Yet still I obeyed and started to sweep away every day.

Then one morning, I felt a divine urgency to speak while sweeping. I began declaring with every stroke of the broom: "God is going to sweep you out of my life, out of my home, just as I am sweeping here. There will be no alarm, no argument and no chaos but just a clean sweep."

I did this faithfully for months and it became like a form of prophetic intercession. My sweeping became my prayer, it became like a warfare chant, and my sweeping became my release.

Then one day it happened, the one who had long refused to change came home and said nothing and began to pack. There was no yelling, no drama and no form of resistance. It felt just like the sweeping had come to an end. God had moved quietly and in his sovereignly, just as He said.

You may feel stuck, like nothing is shifting, but God might already be moving. What feels like repetition or routine may actually be the pattern of your release. Listen for God's instructions and if it is to sweep, just obey and start sweeping, if it is to pray, just obey and keep praying, because He sees and he knows, and when the time comes, it will be clean, complete and covered by His hand.

Reflection

What ordinary task might God be using to work something extraordinary in my life?

Have I obeyed a simple instruction that carries spiritual weight?

Prayer

Lord, teach me to obey even when Your instructions seem small or strange. Help me to trust that You are working behind the scenes, sweeping away what no longer belongs and making room for what aligns with Your will. Give me peace in the silence and strength in the waiting. Amen.

Chapter 17

The Sound of Rain: Go Pray Again

1 Kings 18:41 (KJV)
"And Elijah said unto Ahab, Get thee up, eat and drink; for there is a sound of abundance of rain".

The **sound of rain does not always come with thunder, but when God speaks even silence becomes a promise waiting to pour.**

It was the morning of the prayer conference, I walked into a room cloaked in what felt like a mix of reverence and heaviness to me, a quiet atmosphere where you could almost feel the weight people were carrying, yet the reverence overshadowed much of that.

I had spent more than two weeks prayerfully preparing a message based on what God had shown me through the life of Elijah it was entitled, "There is a sound of abundance of Rain". It was a message of breakthrough, of hope and the assurance that delay is not denial.

As I spoke, midway through the message, the Holy Spirit spoke to me, not with a loud voice or a spectacle, but with a quiet, clear instruction: "Stop and share this: There is someone here who have prayed and prayed, and because they have seen no change, they have stopped. Tell them, pray again, continue to pray."

I paused, and there were no fear and no hesitation, just a holy urgency so I delivered the word. I looked out into the audience and said exactly what I heard. This was a sure word, not mistaken and a matching word from straight from Luke 18, where the story is told of the unjust judge and the woman who sat at his doorstep, unwilling to stop coming until justice was finally given.

Should we not, as God's children, keep praying even when results are not yet seen? For persistence in prayer is not just determination but it is faith that trusts God in the silence, believing that He hears and sees, and He responds in His perfect time."

After the session, a young woman approached me, her eyes wide with astonishment. "That message was for me," she said, almost in a whispered tone, almost speechless. "When you said it, you were looking straight at me. I have a long-standing illness, and I have prayed for years, and nothing has changed. I got so tired and discouraged, so I stopped praying.

In that moment, she heard the call again, "Pray again." God had not forgotten and heaven had heard. The silence did not mean she was discarded but it was a set up. The clouds were forming, and the sound of rain was coming.

You may be like that young woman, worn out from praying, tired of hoping, quietly wondering if God still hears you. Maybe you have stopped asking because it hurts too much to believe again. Now today, hear this, God sees you, God hears you and He is not finished. This is your word, pray again because the clouds are gathering, and the sound of rain is near.

Reflection

Have I allowed delay to silence my prayers?

What promise have I buried that God is now asking me to believe for again?

Prayer

Lord, I confess where I have grown weary in prayer. Remind me that You are the God who hears, even in the waiting. Breathe fresh faith into my soul. Help me to rise, pray again, and wait with expectation, so that I can hear the sound of abundance of rain. Amen.

Chapter 18

What Are You Doing Here?

1 Kings 19:9 (KJV)
"And he came thither unto a cave, and lodged there; and, behold, the word of the LORD came to him, and he said unto him, What doest thou here, Elijah"?

When God asks you where you are, it is not because He does not know but because He wants you to realize you are not where you belong.

Have you ever had a persistent, almost nagging feeling that you were in the wrong place? It may not be geographical but spiritual, emotional or even professional.

I took a job because I needed to work and the bills were real while the pressure was mounting. I convinced myself that "all things work together for good," and that surely God would use this position for something. Yet even with that reasoning, the prompting never left, it was almost constant, quiet at first but growing louder with time.

Then one day, I heard it clearly, almost audibly, "What are you doing here?" It was sharp and it felt like a rebuke, but it was also filled with care, like a parent stopping a child from walking into danger.

In that moment, I realized I had settled, that I had forgotten that while God does use everything for good, He never asked me to ignore His voice. I took that job out of fear, not faith. I did not stop to remember that God always provides, and that sometimes He simply says, "wait."

The job did not bring me peace instead it brought a heavy weight. I was feeling depressed, lost even and sometimes more financially strained than when I was unemployed and not to mention how I felt completely out of alignment. The longer I stayed, the worse I felt until I finally decided to leave.

For me, leaving that job did not mean failure, it meant obedience. I knew I had to heed the call to find my place, because staying where God did not assign me was doing more damage than trusting Him in the unknown.

You too may be feeling the tug, a quiet nudge, or maybe a loud inner voice asking, "What are you doing here?" Do not ignore it. God does not ask questions to condemn you, He asks them to call you into purpose because sometimes staying is harder and costlier than leaving.

Reflection

Is there a situation in your life where God may be asking, "What are you doing here?"

What fears are keeping you in a place that faith might be calling you to leave?

Prayer

Father, help me to discern Your voice above the noise of fear, pressure, and self-reliance. When I am in places You have not called me to be, give me the strength to walk away. Remind me that obedience is better than comfort and that You will never lead me into emptiness, but always into purpose. In Jesus' name, Amen.

Chapter 19

When Are You Going to Obey?

Job 33:14 (KJV)
"For God speaketh once, yea twice, yet man perceiveth it not".

God's voice is soft, but it is the most powerful in a lifetime. The more we hear it, the more familiar we become with it, and the more transformed lives are when we respond.

One of the major questions of many people on their spiritual journey is this: How do I know when God is speaking to me? Some may listen for thunder and signs, and do not know that it is mostly a quiet voice, soft but compelling. I have come to know that voice, and one day I heard that voice, it was a mild but with a very clear whisper within me saying: "Give, Simon (not his real name), a certain amount of money" It was not a small amount not for someone like me, still trying to bounce back from a recent loss. So I dismissed it, thinking it must be a passing thought, maybe even my own imagination.

Days passed and a week, then two weeks and suddenly the voice spoke again, but this time it was stronger and in the form of a question: When will you give Simon the money? It was not scary but it was authoritative, yes, but not angry. The voice sounded like a father who pushes his child toward responsibility, so out of reverence, I called my best friend and shared what I had heard. Her response was simple: "Do what He says."

So we searched for Simon and with a few details that he was a man of God who preached on occasions but was not very well known to me. We found him at a time that was divinely perfect; when I revealed to him God's words, he explained that his need at that time was the exact amount that he needed to fulfil an obligation and had prayed to God earnestly not to bring him to shame. He said he had not told anyone; he had simply prayed about it.

On that day, I learned something awesomely powerful: God was not trying to burden me with the request, but He was looking for a channel to bless someone through me. My obedience was just not about me but part of someone else's deliverance.

You too may be wrestling with a gentle whisper that will not leave you alone. Maybe God is asking you to give, to reach out, to forgive or to act. You do not need to be 100% sure it is Him to begin responding. Begin with respect and start with prayer then trust that obedience opens the doors that can never be opened by logic. What if your yes is someone else's breakthrough?

Reflection

Have you ever sensed God speaking but hesitated because it did not make sense or felt inconvenient?

How can you grow in recognizing and responding to God's voice, even in small matters?

Prayer

Lord, teach me to recognize Your voice not just in thunder, but in whispers. Give me the courage to respond, even when it stretches me or makes no sense to my natural mind. Help me to trust that my obedience matters, not just for me, but for those You want to reach through me. Use me, Lord. In Jesus' name, Amen.

Chapter 20

What Are You Carrying?

Galatians 6:4-5 (NIV)
"Each one should test their own actions. Then they can take pride in themselves alone, without comparing themselves to someone else, for each one should carry their own load".

The true assignment is not always loud, but it is always purposeful.

Not every load we carry is assigned by God because some burdens are self-accepted while others are quietly handed to us by voices, expectations or unhealthy attachments.

During my school days, we had a lot of assignments. We had to solve problems, answer questions and really think hard. The assignments came with deadlines and consequences if we did not finish on time. I often found them tough and would ask why our teachers seemed to pile on the work on us and to add to that, my mom took them very seriously.

Every evening when we got home, she would ask, "Do you have homework?", and before we could even think about relaxing or having fun, she made sure we got our assignments done. Looking back, I realized she understood something I did not at the time. Those assignments were not meant to be a punishment, but they were there to get us ready for the future.

When I reflect on those assignments now, the ones I am talking about today are not the ones written in notebooks or marked with red ink like our teachers did. These are the unseen assignments we carry inside us, often influenced by the voices we hear, our self-belief, and the relationships we maintain. Some of these come from God and are based on purpose and truth. Others stem from fear, guilt, or expectations we have inherited that do not help us anymore.

It is time to ask yourself: Who gave me that assignment? That anxiety? That obligation? That identity? Like my mother standing at the gate, the Holy Spirit gently asks us each day: "Have you checked your assignments?" Not just the ones written, but the ones weighing down your soul.

Reflection

What burden are you carrying today that God may not have assigned to you?

How can you discern between a divine assignment and an unhealthy attachment?

Prayer

Heavenly Father please reveal to me what I have taken on that was not meant for me. Unload my spirit from the unnecessary weight of words, roles and relationships that hinder Your purpose. Help me embrace only what You assign with grace, courage and clarity. In Jesus name Amen.

Chapter 21

The Walk That Changed Everything

Jeremiah 33:3 (NIV)
"Call to me and I will answer you and tell you great and unsearchable things you do not know".

God often speaks the loudest in the quiet places and when you walk with Him long enough, the veil between the seen and unseen begins to lift.

It began like any other morning, it was the kind of morning no one would label as sacred, and yet in heaven, it had already been marked as such.

As was my custom, I took my usual morning walk. Sometimes I walk one mile, sometimes three but on this particular morning, something in the atmosphere had shifted. The air felt heavy with presence, it felt holy not burdensome.

It was not a feeling, it was real. Later that day, I settled into my usual routine, then ran some errands with my sister and daughter, but I noticed that the same lingering presence followed me like a quiet whisper.

Then it happened as we exited a store, something within me crossed over. I was no longer just in the natural, I had stepped into the spiritual. I looked around and saw people walking through the parking lot, but not as you would expect. It was like watching souls in confusion, almost bumping into each other face-first as if there was no direction, no awareness but just noise and chaos in motion.

It was not physical; it was spiritual blindness. A mass of movement without purpose. I turned to my sisters and shouted, "Everyone is bumping into each other, don't you see it?" They stared at me in shock, they saw people, but not what I saw. I had been shown something different.

That was the morning everything changed, my calling, my purpose, my ministry. It was a divine shift, a pulling back of the curtain. God will give you a glimpse of what others could not yet see, not to isolate you, but to activate something in you. When you walk in obedience, He reveals things not to scare you, but to prepare you. He allows you to feel the burden so you can carry the assignment.

This was more than a walk, it was a calling wrapped in clarity. So today I encourage you to be intentional about your walk, both physically and spiritually and tune your heart to God's presence. Do not dismiss the feeling, it may be the setting for a divine encounter. Ask Him to open your eyes to what He is showing you, even if others do not see it yet.

Reflection

Have you ever sensed a moment where God was showing you something others could not perceive? What did you do with that revelation?

Are you walking through life with purpose or are you just moving?

What would it look like to walk with God daily?

Prayer

Father, thank You for walking with me even when I do not recognize the sacredness of the moment. Open my eyes to see beyond the natural into the spiritual truths You are revealing. Help me to embrace my calling, no matter how unfamiliar or misunderstood it may seem. Give me the courage to walk boldly in purpose, and the grace to carry what You have entrusted to me. In Jesus' name, Amen.

Chapter 22

Washer Fluid Wisdom

Proverbs 3:5–6 (NIV)
"Trust in the Lord with all your heart and lean not on your own understanding; in all your ways submit to him, and he will make your paths straight."

The Holy Spirit does not just guide us in grand moments. He whispers wisdom in the ordinary, showing us what we would never know on our own.

It was the heart of winter in New York, very cold and icy and a world away from the warmth of the southern state I had just left. Snowflakes kissed the windshield of my car and the roads bore the scars of a long winter season. I had made it safely to my destination, but my car was not adapting as quickly as I had.

When I started the engine, the windshield was so frosted that I could barely see through it. Naturally as anyone would do, I reached for the washer fluid and turned it on, but nothing came out; there was no spray and no clearing but just a murky view and a worsening chill.

I came out and popped the hood and checked for washer fluid. Sure enough I found half a bottle of blue fluid in the trunk which was standard washer fluid that I had picked up before leaving my warm state. Just as I was about to pour it in my friend stopped me.

"That is not going to work here," he said. You need the winter formula; this one will freeze up in the lines." I was stunned by what he was talking about; washer fluid was not something I would have ever given much thought to because it is just washer fluid. Yet in this new environment, my usual formula would not cut it. I needed something designed for the cold, something that would not freeze up under pressure.

And just like that it hit me; how often do we try to operate in a "new season" using what worked in the last one? What sustained us in one place might not be enough for where God is taking us next. In warmer seasons, maybe we relied on knowledge, or experience, or just sheer momentum. Yet spiritually speaking, winter demands something more. It demands a different formula, deeper wisdom and that is where the Holy Spirit comes in.

Just as my friend stopped me from pouring the wrong fluid into my car, the Holy Spirit often whispers in moments we would dismiss as mundane. His direction is not always loud, but it is always timely, if we are listening. He knows when the old will not work in the new and He nudges us toward the wisdom we would not choose on our own.

The right fluid made all the difference, and my washer system came back to life, the windshield was cleared with ease. What had been stuck, frozen and ineffective began to function the way it was designed to.

So, it is with us, when we lean into the Holy Spirit's guidance, we find that we are not just surviving the season, we are moving through it with clarity and purpose.

Reflection

Are there "old season" habits or mindsets that you are trying to carry into a new spiritual season?

In what area of your life is the Holy Spirit inviting you to seek fresh wisdom or direction?

Prayer

Holy Spirit, thank You for being my guide in every season. Teach me to listen for Your voice, even in the small things. Help me let go of what no longer serves me and embrace the wisdom You provide for where I am now. I trust You to lead me, clear my vision, and prepare me for the road ahead. In Jesus' name, amen.

Chapter 23

Too Heavy for the Load

Matthew 11:28 (NIV)
"Come to me, all you who are weary and burdened, and I will give you rest".

Just because you can fit it in does not mean you are built to carry it; some loads were never meant to be managed alone.

There was a season of my life when I lived in a small apartment with a washer and dryer compact enough to fit the space and perfect for light clothes and a simple load but it was not designed for anything too large.

From as far back as I can remember, I have always had a love for big, fluffy bedspreads. The kind that almost breathes life into a room. I would take a moment each morning to admire how they made the entire bed look so fluffy like a cloud, so inviting, elegant and comforting. Yet when I think about washing them, that was a different story.

One summer, I bought a new bedspread and thought surely this one was not as big as the others. I convinced myself it would fit in my little washer so I stuffed it in just barely and shut the lid. To my delight, the machine started humming along as if everything was fine. There were no unusual sounds and no warning lights so I smiled, thinking I would finally figure out how to manage the big stuff from home.

Then came the rinse cycle and when the machine started to wring out the water, that comforter turned into a heavy, unbalanced burden. The washer began to rock violently, slamming against the floor, with a struggling sound echoing through the apartment. Instantly panic replaced my pride and accomplishment, so I quickly ran and shut it off. Later I had to pull it out soaking wet and twice as heavy and carried it to a nearby laundromat to finish the job.

I learned something valuable that day and that was not because something fits, it does not mean it belongs there. We often treat life the same way when we try to carry burdens we were never meant to carry alone. We stuff emotional weight, responsibilities and even relationships into spaces in our hearts and minds that were never built for them.

For a while things may seem fine but as we move forward and we function we realize the burden is more that we can bear. When life hits the rinse cycle at the pressure point, everything will start to shake; and just like my little washer, we may find ourselves overwhelmed, overburdened and making noise no one can ignore. That is when God will gently reminds us, "You were never meant to carry this by yourself."

There was nothing wrong with the comforter, it just needed a bigger machine and there is nothing wrong with you, but you need the strength only God can provide. He invites us to bring our oversized burdens to Him, to stop forcing what does not fit and trust that He has already made provision for the heavy things.

Reflection

What burden are you currently trying to carry in your own strength that may be too heavy for you alone?

In what area is God asking you to release control and bring the weight to Him?

Prayer

Lord, help me to recognize when I am carrying more than I was made to bear. Teach me to trust You with the heavy things, the emotions, the responsibilities, the expectations. Thank You that I do not have to force what does not fit. You are strong enough, big enough, and faithful enough to carry what I cannot. In Jesus' name, amen.

Chapter 24

The Quiet Strength of Faith

Deuteronomy 31:6 (NIV)
"Be strong and courageous. Do not be afraid or terrified because of them, for the Lord your God goes with you; He will never leave you nor forsake you".

Faith is not always loud, it can sit quietly in the soul, sure and unmoved, even when the world shakes.

My father was not the easiest man to get along with or close to. He was stern, sometimes loud at other times he would be quiet as a man of few words, but he had deep presence. Though he never professed to be a Christian or follow Christ in any way, he carried within him an unusual depth of wisdom, almost seeming prophetic at times.

There were moments when he would speak of things before they happened, not as if he were guessing, but with the calm confidence of someone who knew. One thing I noticed about him was that fear never seemed to bother him or touch him.

I don't think it was so much arrogance, but it was something else, because he seem to have had a sense of discernment, especially about the spiritual. If there were evil forces near, he would know. Not only would he know, but he would also confront them directly, fearlessly, sending them away with words sharp as steel.

One day, in his old-fashioned, determined way, he decided he would not wait for the younger men to come and climb the tall coconut tree that stood in our yard, laden with fruit. Without asking for help he climbed the tree but before he could reach the top he fell right down to the ground.

We rushed to him, expecting the worst but when we got to him he stood up, dusted off himself and looked calm and completely at peace. There were no broken bones and no fear in his eyes. He insisted not to be taken to the doctor. "I'll be fine," he said, "This won't kill me." and it did not. He lived to ninety-two years and never needing to see a doctor for anything related to that fall.

I still remember the words to my sister from one of the nurses who worked at the hospital where he spent his final two days before leaving earth. "Was your father a Christian, as he sang several worship songs until his last breath."

His life reminds me that faith does not always wear the garments of religion, sometimes faith looks like my father, a man who walked so fearlessly through life because he knows, deep down that all is well and that God is present.

Unlike my father I am a Christian and many people look at me and say "you are so strong and fearless" but they may not know that I still struggle with fear and doubt sometimes. At other times, I question the outcomes, and I even worry and hold back at times.

Yet every day I am growing more and more in my faith, and now when I remember my father, I am reminded that faith is not about the noise we make in prayer or in church, but the certainty we carry; that stillness that refuses to be shaken.

Reflection

What does fearless faith look like in your daily life and what holds you back from walking in it?

How can you cultivate a deeper assurance in God's presence, even when circumstances try to shake you?

Prayer

Dear Lord, please help me to walk with unwavering trust, even when the road is uncertain. Teach me to be still in my spirit, strong in my faith, and unshaken by fear. May I sense Your presence more clearly and trust

Your leading more deeply. Like my father, may I live in quiet courage, knowing that You are always with me. In Jesus name Amen.

Chapter 25

The Road to Resilience

Romans 5:3-4 (NIV)
"Not only so, but we also glory in our sufferings, because we know that suffering produces perseverance; perseverance, character; and character, hope."

Resilience is not built in comfort, but in the quiet places where faith walks hand in hand with endurance.

A young man shared with me how he left his home country to start a new life in the United States. It was winter when he arrived, cold and unfamiliar. He found work quickly but it came at a cost because he had to do long hours, with no breaks and sometimes seven-day weeks with late-night bus rides home in the freezing dark.

Despite the discomfort and loneliness, he said he never once thought about quitting. When he told me that, I said to him, "You were traveling the road to resilience."

This story reminds me of Joseph in the Bible how he was betrayed by his brothers, sold into slavery and falsely accused then thrown into prison. Joseph faced hardship after hardship, but never once did he give up. He remained faithful, resilient and hopeful in God. In time he rose to become second-in-command in Egypt, saving nations from famine.

Just like Joseph, this young man held on through the storm, and now he has a job he loves, works regular hours and is thriving. His story is a testament that resilience is not just about enduring but it is about trusting that God is shaping our character through it.

So, if you are traveling the road to resilience, know that God is not punishing you, He is preparing you. Every difficult moment is a steppingstone toward the person you are becoming. Do not despise the season you are in; it is producing something eternal.

Reflection

What season are you in at this time that is causing you to probably doubt God?

In what ways can you live out a quiet resilience in ways that please God?

Prayer

Dear Lord, when the road gets hard and the nights feel long, help me to remember that You are with me. Strengthen my heart, build my character, and help me to trust that my resilience is part of Your plan. In Jesus name Amen.

Chapter 26

Hidden in Plain Sight

Nehemiah 6:3 (KJV)
"And I sent messengers unto them, saying, I *am* doing a great work, so that I cannot come down: why should the work cease, whilst I leave it, and come down to you?"

Some hands offer help, but their hearts carry hidden agendas. Discernment is how you protect the assignment God gave you.

At one of my places of employment, we strive to stand for teamwork, we show up for one another, lend a hand and try to keep things running smoothly and that is what I believed until one day.

A team member offered to help on a project and though I did not really need it, I agreed because that is what team players do, right? The outcome was a disaster and the help led to a major deviation from the plan, and I was left cleaning up the mess and explaining the shortfall.

It was not just a professional mistake; it was a personal revelation because I realized that not all help is holy and not everyone who offers help does so with a pure heart. Some have hidden motives, competition, control or even the desire to be seen as superior.

This reminds me of Nehemiah's story, as he led the rebuilding of Jerusalem's walls, opposition came not just from enemies, but from people who pretended to want to help. In Nehemiah 6, two men like Sanballat and Tobiah tried to lure him into distraction under the disguise that they would work together. Nehemiah observed their motives and told them, "I am doing a great work, and I cannot come down." He said this because he understood something vital and that was, not every offer of help is sent by God.

In life, ministry and leadership, the wrong kind of help can delay your destiny, drain your energy and derail your focus. On the other hand, the right kind of help, the God-ordained, pure-hearted and purpose-driven help can push you forward into your divine assignment.

Later I learnt about these five types of people, and this makes much sense as I read them. Hope it will be for you too.

Destiny Pushers – They are sent by God to align with your purpose and elevate your calling.

Silent Strengths – They may never ask for praise, but they are consistent, loyal and dependable.

Strategic Allies – These people come into your life and the relationships are equally beneficial and is rooted in trust and value.

Hidden Hijackers – Their help is a trap to control and manipulate you, look out for them and steer clear of them.

Glory Seekers – Their main interest is to be seen by others and not so much to work towards you gaining victory.

This week, ask God for spiritual discernment do not just see what people do ask for wisdom to perceive why they are doing it. Then examine the hearts that work behind the hands. You have a purpose to fulfill and not everyone deserves access to your mission.

Prayer

Father, thank You for being my constant help and source of wisdom. I ask for sharp discernment in this season. Help me to recognize pure motives and distance myself from deception. Surround me with destiny pushers and reveal the hearts of those not aligned with Your will for my life. I trust You to guide me and protect what You have called me to build. In Jesus' name, Amen.

Chapter 27

God had another Chapter in Mind

Isaiah 43:18–19 (NIV)
"Forget the former things; do not dwell on the past. See, I am doing a new thing! Now it springs up; do you not perceive it? I am making a way in the wilderness and streams in the wasteland".

God rarely calls us to comfort He calls us to obedience, where new oil is pressed and purpose is revealed.

My journey towards a spiritual shift started with the regular tasks which I loved. For over twenty years, I was faithfully planted in my local church and it was more than a place of worship, it was more like home.

During those years, I served on at least nine committees. I taught Sunday School, Sunday after Sunday, prayers, served on the pastoral committee and was involved in just about every area you could think of. You could say I was one of the "head cook and bottle washer."

Everyone knew my name and face, even if I could not always remember theirs. Out of a congregation of about fifteen hundred members, I knew many and many knew me. I felt rooted, purposeful and was certain that this was where I would serve indefinitely. I thought the assignment would stay the same.

Then the assignment shifted and unexpectedly the rhythm changed. I began to feel unsettled not because I no longer loved serving, but because something in my spirit was shifting, something felt awkward. I started to second-guess everything. Was this really God? Why now? What would people think?

Then one day, a seasoned church mother approached me quietly and said with conviction, "You need to go now." I did not doubt that she was hearing from God and trusted that these words were the confirmation I had been wrestling with. In a short time, I packed up my comfort and stepped into unfamiliar territory, into another country, another context and another calling.

Stay tune for the part two coming up in the next chapter when the assignment changed and I had to make a decision whether to trust God for the next.

Reflection

Have I become so comfortable in my current assignment that I am resisting God's call to move?

What fears or uncertainties are holding me back from stepping into the unknown with faith?

Prayer

Father, thank You for every season of service You have walked me through. Thank You for the growth, the memories, the relationships, and the joy of serving where I once was. But now, Lord, I sense You doing something new. Give me the courage to follow You away from comfort and into calling. Help me not to cling to what was, but to embrace what is yet to come. Let my life be a vessel for Your voice, and my hands a tool for Your purpose. In Jesus' name, Amen.

Chapter 28

The Redefined Assignment

Part II
Isaiah 43:18–19 (NIV)

"Forget the former things; do not dwell on the past. See, I am doing a new thing! Now it springs up; do you not perceive it? I am making a way in the wilderness and streams in the wasteland".

I thought the assignment would stay the same but God had another chapter in mind.

There was a ripple effect of obedience, my move was less than glamorous and was nothing near what I had anticipated. There was no grand welcome and no clear path because everything felt and looked "less" in the natural. Yet this season became the most spiritually rich season of my life.

In this new place, away from the crowd and the committees, God began to redefine my assignment. I moved into a seer ministry; I spoke as God gave utterance, I prayed prayers for healing and blessing, wrote and published my first book and I counseled and coached with insight that only the Holy Spirit could give me each time.

The assignment I once feared, became the most fruitful season of my walk with Christ. Looking back now I would not change a thing.

It was in the unfamiliar that God sharpened my spiritual senses. It was away from the noise, that He awakened the gifts I did not know were lying dormant. Like Abraham, I had to leave what was familiar to receive the fullness of the promise. Like Philip, I had to move from the crowd to a desert road only to realize it was a divine setup.

In what appeared to aloneness, God was not punishing me He was promoting me, but only on His terms, not mine. I learned that God does not just assign us to places; but He assigns us to purposes and when the place shifts the purpose deepens.

Maybe you are sensing a shift too, maybe your assignment is changing, and it scares you. Let me encourage you, do not fight the move. Do not let the comfort of the familiar rob you of the depth that comes through obedience.

When God redirects your path, it is never to diminish your purpose, it is to unlock a greater version of it.

Reflection

Have I become so comfortable in my current assignment that I am resisting God's call to move?

What fears or uncertainties are holding me back from stepping into the unknown with faith?

Prayer

Father, thank You for every season of service You have walked me through. Thank You for the growth, the memories, the relationships, and the joy of serving where I once was. But now, Lord, I sense You doing something new. Give me the courage to follow You away from comfort and into calling. Help me not to cling to what was, but to embrace what is yet to come. Let my life be a vessel for Your voice, and my hands a tool for Your purpose. In Jesus' name, Amen.

Chapter 29

Trust What You See?

Hebrews 11:1 (KJV
"Now faith is the substance of things hoped for, the evidence of things not seen".

Sometimes God does not tell us the time, He shows us the clock. Faith means believing even when He does not speak.

My sister once lived in one of the remote countryside where transportation is limited. One day, while waiting endlessly for a taxi to the city, she lost track of time. With no phone or watch on her, she turned to the man next to *her,* who wore a striking gold watch.

"Excuse me, sir, do you know the time?" she asked. He glanced down at his wrist and then extended his arm toward her saying, "You read it for yourself because if I tell you, you will not believe me."

That simple interaction left an impression on me. I could not help but wonder; was it that he could not read the watch himself? Or was the time so surprising that he thought no one would believe it?

In our walk with God, there are moments when He holds out His "watch" to us. Instead of telling us everything plainly, He invites us to look, discern and trust. Maybe the answer is in front of us, but we have grown so accustomed to hearing instead of seeking and seeing.

God does not always give us the timeline in words, sometimes He shows us in ways that require faith to interpret through delays, closed doors, unexpected encounters, or even silence.

Is God showing you something right now that you have been waiting for Him to say? Step back, look again, and ask for discernment. Do not miss His answer because it is not delivered in the way you expected.

Reflection

Have you ever missed what God was showing you because you were waiting to hear it instead?

What is one area in your life where God might be calling you to trust what you see with spiritual eyes?

Prayer

Lord, open my eyes to see what You are showing me. Teach me to trust Your timing, even when I do not hear Your voice clearly. Help me to grow in faith and discernment, so I do not miss the answers that are right before me. In Jesus name Amen.

Chapter 30

Too Good to Be God?

1 John 4:1 (KJV)
"Beloved, do not believe every spirit, but test the spirits, whether they are of God; because many false prophets have gone out into the world".

Not every open door is God's will, some are painted to look like blessings but lead straight into traps.

Some years ago, I decided to look for a second source of income. With a bit of savings set aside, I began exploring different investment opportunities. An acquaintance told me about a "sure deal" involving the resale of used cars, promising 50 to 100 percent returns. At first, it sounded too good to be true, and something in me hesitated. Yet he kept coming back, persuading me with stories of quick profits.

Eventually, I went against my better judgment and sent someone I trusted to inspect the car that had been bought with my money. When the person saw it, his words hit hard: "Did you pick that out of a garbage heap?" The deal was a scam because the car could not be resold, and the person behind the scheme had no intention of refunding the money.

In that moment, I realized this was not just a financial misstep, but it was also a spiritual lesson. I ignored the internal prompting, the unease that whispered, "This isn't right." I let the voice of persuasion drown out the voice of discernment. I thought I was dealing with people, but in truth, I was in a battle of spirits, one where wisdom, patience and spiritual alertness are essential.

God often gives us warning signs, not always through flashing lights or loud voices, but through gentle checks in our spirit. When we override those promptings for the promise of quick gain, we can find ourselves trapped in regret. Yet even then, God is merciful and He teaches us through our losses and uses them to build spiritual maturity in us.

Before making any decision, especially one that seems too good to be true, pause and pray, then invite the Holy Spirit to guide you. Do not override the red flags because God's voice brings peace and not pressure.

Reflection

Can you recall a time when you felt uneasy about a decision but moved forward anyway? What was the result?

How can you strengthen your ability to discern God's voice in daily decisions?

Prayer

Lord, help me to listen when You speak especially when the truth is quiet and the lies are loud. Teach me to trust Your wisdom above my own desires. Guard my heart from deception and my discernment so that I may walk in truth and peace. In Jesus name Amen.

Chapter 31

When Gratitude Supersedes

1 Thessalonians 5:18 (KJV)
"In everything give thanks; for this is the will of God in Christ Jesus concerning you".

Gratitude is not about what you have, it is about what you carry inside you.

Little Joel was walking when he noticed an old man sitting quietly by the roadside. Curious, he asked, "Why are you sitting here?" The man smiled and said, "I am here because I have life, and I am thankful."

Joel looked at the man's two small bags beside him. There was no fancy car, no fancy clothes, nothing that most would consider a blessing. Joel could not understand how someone in such a humble and yet desperate state could be thankful just to be alive.

As he walked on, Joel stumbled into a small crowd. A minor car accident had occurred two men were yelling over barely scratched vehicles. Joel, still thinking of the old man, said, "Why are you fussing? You are alive, and your cars can be repaired. There is a man is sitting by the roadside just a mile away, smiling and thankful for life."

One of the men snapped back, "Move on, little lad! My vehicle is more important than anything to me." That day, Joel saw two drastically different ways to live: one man, with almost nothing, carried gratitude. Another, with much, carried anger and entitlement.

Gratitude is not about how much we have, but how much we recognize. Sometimes those who seem to have the least are the richest in spirit, and sometimes, those who seem to have everything live in emotional and spiritual poverty.

The old man's two small bags might not have held much, but his heart was full. Full of life and full of thanks; that is what made him truly rich. Pause today and ask: What are you truly carrying? Are you weighed down by what you do not have, or lifted by what you *do*? Gratitude is a decision so choose it, regardless of your situation.

Reflection

Have you ever found yourself being ungrateful even when you had more than enough? What caused the shift in perspective?

What "small" blessings in your life have you been overlooking?

Prayer

Lord, teach me to be thankful, not because

everything is perfect, but because You are present. Help me carry gratitude no matter my circumstances and open my eyes to the simple blessings! In Jesus name Amen

Chapter 32

Strong but Struggling

2 Corinthians 12:9 (KJV)
"And he said unto me, My grace is sufficient for thee: for my strength is made perfect in weakness. Most gladly therefore will I rather glory in my infirmities, that the power of Christ may rest upon me".

True strength is not the absence of weakness, but the choice to carry others even when you are uncertain of yourself.

John my friend lived in a small town, and everyone knows him as he is a bodybuilder, lifting weights for years. Many call him the "champion of weights," and some even call him "Iron Man." John can lift a hundred-pound weight with ease, his physical power is undeniable.

Walking with John, you feel safe, because he is like a wall of strength. People in the town rely on him, not just for his muscle strength but as their sense of protection because his presence makes others feel secure.

Yet what most people do not know is that deep down John carries insecurities. Sometimes he would quietly ask, "What if I don't live up to what they expect from me?" Even with these doubts, he continues to show up, to stand tall and to be a symbol of strength for his community.

John reminds me that even the strongest people have silent battles. What we see on the outside does not always reflect the storm inside. Yet God has a way of using broken, burdened people to be vessels of strength to carry out his mission.

The beauty of grace is that God does not wait for us to be perfect before He uses us. His strength shines brightest when we admit our weakness. Like John, you do not have to feel strong to be strong. You just have to show up and let God fill the gaps.

Are you carrying others while quietly battling your own insecurities? Are you ashamed of your inner struggle? Then bring it to God because His grace will sustain you, and His strength will be made perfect through you.

Reflection

Have you ever felt pressured to appear strong for others even when you were struggling inside? How did it affect you?

What would it look like to trust God with your hidden insecurities today?

Prayer

Father, thank You for being strong when I feel

weak. I surrender the pressure to be everything for everyone. Remind me that I can be used by You, not because I have no flaws, but because You are faithful. Be my strength when I feel unsure. In Jesus name Amen.

Chapter 33

When the Spirit Says Move

Ezekiel 1:20 (NIV)
"Wherever the Spirit would go, they would go, and the wheels would rise alongside them, because the spirit of the living creatures was in the wheels".

Obedience does not always come with clarity. Sometimes it just comes with a whisper strong enough to move your feet.

Sometime ago, I felt something in my spirit that I could not shake. It was not a casual thought or a fleeting feeling. It felt like it was a divine summons, an unspoken yet undeniably loud voice as if God was calling me to move from where I was physically, spiritually and in faith.

There was no job waiting and funds were tight, yet the call was clear in my mind that this was the time. No one else could see the path, but I could feel it and the timing felt sacred, like a window that would not stay open long.

So, without explanation or fanfare, I started packing my things. I did not broadcast it to anyone because I have learned that not everyone will understand your assignment. Sometimes other people's doubts can fog up what God has made crystal clear in your spirit.

Ezekiel 1:20 paints a picture of an obedient, Spirit-led movement. The creatures moved only when the Spirit moved, and the wheels rose only when the Spirit lifted them. It was divine alignment, perfect timing and a movement governed by heaven.

That sounded like what I experienced because there was no blueprint, just a call to obedience. There were no guarantees as to what lay ahead, but I just needed to trust. The one thing that stood out was that peace followed every step, confirming what logic could not. The move went just as God needed it to be.

So, if you feel a divine nudge do not ignore it. Do not wait for the whole map when God is simply saying, take the next step. Do not let fear of missing out keep you from stepping into what God is preparing.

Just listen, trust, and move because your obedience today could unlock your breakthrough tomorrow.

Reflection

Have I ever ignored a prompting from the Holy Spirit because it did not make logical sense or seemed too risky? What held me back, and what might have happened if I had obeyed?

What next step might the Spirit be asking me to take right now, even if I do not see the full picture? How can I prepare my heart to respond with faith and obedience?

Prayer

Father, teach me to move when You move. Even when I do not understand, give me the faith to trust your timing. Silence the voices of doubt and distraction and sharpen my ear to hear Yours. May I never miss my moment because I waited for perfect clarity. Let Your Spirit lead, and I will follow. In Jesus' name, Amen.

Chapter 34

Waiting for the Ripening

James 1:4 (KJV)

"But let patience have her perfect work, that ye may be perfect and entire, wanting nothing".

Impatience hides what we are not ready to receive, but patience reveals what God is preparing for us to enjoy.

Growing up, our home was surrounded by fruit trees. Some were so close to the house that we could reach out the window and pick from the branches. Every spring, the wind would shake the trees overnight and in the morning we would run out to see what fruit had fallen.

Then we would gather them joyfully, rinse them off and place them on the table for everyone to enjoy. Our hearts overflowed with thankfulness seeing all that fresh fruit, not just because it was delicious, but because it felt like a gift from heaven.

Then there were also mornings when there was nothing. No ripe fruit had fallen and when that happened, the temptation grew stronger to pick the ones that were not ready. Our father warned us, "Do not pick the green ones and not even touch the half-ripe ones, they need time."

We did not always listen and sometimes we would secretly pick the not-quite-ready fruit and hide it under the bed, hoping it would ripen faster or that no one would notice.

Looking back, I realize how often we do the same with life. We grow impatient waiting on God for provision, breakthrough, healing, relationships and in our rush, we pick what is not ready. Then we hide our decisions, hoping they will ripen outside of God's process.

What is green today may be sweet tomorrow if we wait. God's timing is not just about delay; it is about development. Patience does not just protect the fruit it prepares for the harvest. Are you tempted to force something before it is fully ready? Resist the urge to pick prematurely. Trust that God's timing produces the best fruit sweet, satisfying, and shared in joy.

Reflection

What is one area of your life where you are tempted to rush God's timing?

Have you ever picked something too early and seen the consequences? What did you learn from it?

Reflection:

What is one area of your life where you are tempted to rush God's timing?

Have you ever picked something too early and seen the consequences? What did you learn from it?

Prayer

Lord, give me the patience to wait on what You are preparing. Teach me not to rush or reach for what is not ready. Help me trust that in due season, You will provide all that I need ripe, full, and overflowing. In Jesus name Amen.

Chapter 35

The Answer You Want

John 8:32 (NLT)
"And you will know the truth, and the truth will set you free".
The answers we get may satisfy the mind, but the truth we need should convict the heart.

Growing up, many of us were told to find the right answers on tests papers, in church and in life. We learned quickly that knowing the right thing to say earned approval from others.

We were taught how to sound correct, how to act right and how to answer questions, yet few of us were taught how to slow down, look deeper and seek truth even when it is uncomfortable or unpopular.

The answers we get may satisfy the mind, but the truth we need should convict the heart. Answers may win us many arguments, but truth will transform lives. Nicodemus a well-known biblical figure had to face the truth even though he was only looking for answers.

The story of Nicodemus in John 3 tells us how Nicodemus was a Pharisee and a religious leader, teacher and a scholar. He knew all the right answers to many questions and he also knew the Scriptures and was a keeper of the law

and held a high position in society. Yet something deeper stirred in him when he saw Jesus because he came to Jesus at night with his question, perhaps to avoid being seen by anyone.
He said, "Rabbi, we know that you are a teacher who has come from God. For no one could perform the signs you are doing if God were not with him. (John 3:2). Nicodemus was not expecting Jesus to answer him that way. More than likely, he may have thought Jesus would get into some biblical debate with him or give him some sort of evidence of what he already believed about him so he could feel better that day.

Jesus did not give him the answer he wanted, instead Jesus gave him the truth he needed. Very truly I tell you, no one can see the kingdom of God unless they are born again. (John 3:3). The truth confused Nicodemus as he asked. "How can someone be born when they are old?" Jesus patiently explained spiritual rebirth and how the Spirit moves like the wind, unseen yet powerful and how faith in God, and not knowledge leads to eternal life.

Nicodemus did not walk away with a just the right answer. He walked away with a seed of truth planted in his heart and that is really the truth he needed and that is the same truth that

Reflection

Are you searching for an answer that fits your current view, or are you open to the truth that might change it?

Prayer

Lord Jesus, just as You met Nicodemus in the quiet of the night, meet me in my questions and uncertainties. Shine Your light into the places I don't yet understand and draw me closer to the truth of who You are. Give me a humble, seeking heart, and the courage to follow You fully. In Jesus name Amen."

Chapter 36

The Journey from Knowledge to Truth

John 8:32 (NLT)
And you will know the truth, and the truth will set you free.

The journey from knowledge to truth begins when we stop collecting answers and start questioning ourselves.

Nicodemus was a little man from what we learn about him appearing in the gospels more than once; two times in the Gospel of John and was defending Jesus before his fellow Pharisees in John 7 verse 50 and finally after Jesus' crucifixion, he was helping Joseph of Arimathea bury Jesus' body in John 19 verse 39.

At this point Nicodemus had received the truth as you can imagine, and the truth had taken root. He was no longer a seeker of answers, but a witness to the Truth himself.

What an eye-opening encounter, the searcher for answers had now become the witness to truth of Christ. Isn't that God?

Reflection
Like Nicodemus, we all at some time found ourselves wrestling with the truth we didn't expect?

Let's consider what would it look like to sit with that truth long enough to let it transform you?

Prayer

Dear Lord, I confess that I often chase answers to feel secure or in control. You are not merely the answer to my questions you are the Truth my soul needs. Help me, like Nicodemus, to come to You honestly. Disrupt my comfort if necessary and plant Your truth in me, even when it is hard to understand. Let it grow. Let it change me. In Jesus name Amen.

Chapter 37

When the Wind Changes

Part One

Ecclesiastes 3:1 (KJV)
"To everything there is a season, and a time to every purpose under the heaven".

The cold does not give notice and neither do the seasons of life. But just as we learn to grab a coat, we can learn to prepare our souls.

I had just moved across the country for a fresh start, new energy, a little uncertainty but a whole lot of faith. Back home in my state, the sun was an ever-present personality, steady and familiar. Morning runs were a ritual for me. The kind that helped me shake off worry and wake up the spirit.

Late spring had come, and the night before had been just warm and cozy. It pulled me into thinking this new city might not be so different after all. I tied my shoes, ran down the stairs and pushed open the door.

Then it hit me a right in my face; a gust of bitter, biting wind. I stood there stunned as I was not dressed for this. My thin running shirt and lightweight pants were no match for the cold that had not bothered to give any notice of its arrival.

All I could say was, "Wow." I turned around, ran back upstairs and grabbed my coat. The cold did not give notice and is not that what life is about sometimes?

We are cruising through comfortable seasons, familiar rhythms, easy prayers, manageable problems and then, suddenly, the cold wind of change shows up uninvited. A relationship breaks, a job ends, a diagnosis comes. A move takes you farther than just geographically. And just like that, the warmth is gone.

But here is the truth; the cold did not surprise God, it surprised me and like that morning run, I had a choice to retreat and stay inside forever, or to adapt. This week don't resist the wind. Just reflect on a current or recent cold front in your life. Instead of rushing back inside or giving up, ask God what kind of coat he's offering you. Lean in, layer up and step out because you are not alone in the shift.

Reflection

What cold season have you recently encountered that caught you off guard?

How is God inviting you to prepare, not just to endure change, but to grow through it?

Prayer

Lord, You are faithful in every season. In times of growth, teach me gratitude. In times of waiting, give me patience. In times of change, grant me peace. Whatever season I'm in, help me trust Your steady hand and rest in Your unfailing love. In Jesus name Amen."

Chapter 38

Warmed by the Walk

Part Two:

Matthew 28:20 (KJV)
"And lo, I am with you always, even unto the end of the world".
Life does not always give notice but God always gives grace.

Life does not always give notice, just like that wind in the previous chapter, but God always gives grace. God does not always calm the storm first, but He always equips us to walk through it. Sometimes that may be as simple as grabbing your coat which may represent your spiritual armor, your community, your time in the Word, or simply pausing long enough to pray, "Lord, help me adjust."

God uses the cold to awaken something in us because comfort rarely cultivates growth, but change does. It toughens your resolve. It deepens your reliance. And it reminds you that seasons are temporary, but God is eternal.

The wind may have brightened me, but it can't stop you when you walk with the One who never changes. I stepped outside again, this time with my coat wrapped tight and my resolve a little stronger. The air was still very cold, but something had shifted, not outside but inside me. I had adjusted and I had responded.

As I began to run, something unexpected happened, my body started to warm up. What once felt unbearable became manageable. The chill was still there but I was moving through it. Step by step, breath by breath, I found rhythm again not because the weather changed but because I did.

That is more like the walk that warms us and is not that what God does with us? He doesn't always change our situation right away, but He changes us within it. We often ask God to remove the cold, but more often, He teaches us how to walk through it because it is how we build strength in discomfort, it is how we find joy in uncertainty, and how we discover peace even when nothing around us feels peaceful.

If I had stayed inside that morning, I would have missed the lesson. I would have missed the moment God wanted to show me that growth does not wait for perfect conditions. Sometimes, our greatest spiritual breakthroughs happen when we refuse to let the cold push us back. When we choose to lace up our shoes, cover ourselves in faith and say, let us go, God. I will walk with You.

Then somewhere along the way we warm up, and it does not happen because life got easier, but because His presence became more real, more felt and even more necessary and that is the power of walking with Jesus.

This week I encourage you to keep walking even if the wind is still blowing. Take one faithful step in that area where you have felt resistance or discomfort.

Let that step be your declaration that this cold won't define you, because God doesn't just meet us in the warmth; He walks with us in the chill and always brings warmth with Him.

Reflection

What area of your life have you been waiting for to warm you up before taking action? What step of faith can you take this week, even if the conditions don't feel ideal?

Prayer

Lord, thank You for Your grace that meets me right where I am. When I fall short, lift me up. When I am weak, strengthen me. Help me receive Your grace with a grateful heart and extend that same grace to others. In Jesus name Amen."

Chapter 39

Unseen Stories, Unexpected Grace

Part One:

Hebrews 13:2 (NIV)
"Do not forget to show hospitality to strangers, for by so doing some people have shown hospitality to angels without knowing it".

Sometimes we think others know, but they don't and that is where compassion meets calling.

It was early morning. quiet, peaceful and perfect for getting my laundry done quickly and without distraction. Only a few of us were there at the laundry and I had a plan to get in and out in an hour. Focused on my task, I barely noticed him behind me until he quietly stepped closer and said, "Can you show me how to operate the machine?"

I paused and looked at him; there was no shame in his voice, only honesty. So I did what he needed to be done, I showed him how to load funds onto his card, then walked him over to the washer and gave him a quick lesson. That moment could have been brushed off as small but something about it lingered.

Later, as the room started to fill with more people and it was time to dry my clothes, I saw him again. The same posture and the same humility. "Can you show me how to use the dryer?"

Again, I showed him but this time I smiled and said something from the heart: "I understand, back where we are from, we wash with our hands and pin the clothes on the line out back."

He laughed with recognition, and in that small exchange, something holy passed between us, not just information but understanding. There was no assumption on my part of him having that knowledge, is it not how life is sometimes?

We assume everyone else knows what they are doing. We assume they have been taught and that they have had the same experiences as us and that they are just like us, but sometimes they really do not know.

They are new, they are learning and sometimes they have just arrived in a world that runs on different rules than the one they came from. In those moments, we are given a choice not just to help but to connect. To help them up their learning curve without judgment and to remember where we came from.

That man didn't need someone to just teach him. He needed someone who would see him and is not that exactly what Jesus did?

This week, be aware of someone who might not know what you assume they do. Instead of judging or ignoring, take a moment to share what you have learned. Not to elevate yourself but to lift them.

Because sometimes the most sacred lessons happen in laundromats, grocery stores, lobbies, and quiet places where strangers dare to ask.

Reflection

Have you ever needed help but were afraid to ask? Make notes of some of those times, how did you feel?

Who around you might need more kindness than instruction this week?

Prayer

Lord, thank You for Your grace that meets me right where I am. When I fall short, lift me up. When I am weak, strengthen me. Help me receive Your grace with a grateful heart and extend that same grace to others. In Jesus name Amen."

Chapter 40

Teach Me Gently

Part Two:

Galatians 6:2 (NIV)

"Carry each other's burdens, and in this way you will fulfill the law of Christ".

Kindness is the language that teaches without shaming and uplifts without asking for applause.

I did not know his full story, I did not know if this was his first time in that laundry or his first time in this country. I do not know what it cost him to ask for help, not once, but twice.

Yet I did know what it cost me: a few minutes of my time, those few minutes turned into something eternal, a small moment where dignity was restored instead of taken. I did not give him advice; I gave him space and I did not show off knowledge; I shared what I once had to learn too.

Then it hit me later how many people silently are waiting for someone to show them, not just how to work a machine, but how to walk through life with grace? How many are navigating systems they have never been taught, carrying shame they never asked for, and hiding questions because they are afraid, they will look foolish?

Sometimes people don't need us to be experts, they just need us to be kind. When God puts you in the teacher's seat is not that the essence of discipleship? Not preaching from a stage but quietly walking someone over to the machine and saying, "Here is how I learned to do it." Not holding your knowledge over someone's head, but placing it gently in their hands and saying, "I remember when I did not know either."

Jesus never shamed the ones who did not know. He taught the willing and defended the learning, and now He asks us to do the same, because one day, you were the one asking how and one day, you will be the one someone remembers not for your brilliance but for your gentleness.

This week, pay attention to the people who are quietly watching from the edges, those who may not speak up but need help. Step into your role as a gentle teacher, not because you know everything, but because you remember what it felt like to know nothing. Let your love speak louder than your knowledge.

Reflection

Who in your life might need a "gentle lesson" instead of loud instruction?

What areas have you grown in that you can now share with others from a place of humility?

Prayer

Loving God, teach me gently today. Guide my thoughts with Your wisdom, shape my words with Your kindness, and lead my steps with Your peace. Show me how to grow with grace, to listen with patience, and to love with a humble heart. In Jesus name Amen."

Chapter 41

One Destination, Many Faces

Part 1: The Beauty of Our Differences

Revelation 7:9 (NIV)
After this I looked, and there before me was a great multitude that no one could count, from every nation, tribe, people and language, standing before the throne and before the Lamb. They were wearing white robes and were holding palm branches in their hands.

God paints with every shade, sculpts with every feature and still calls it one masterpiece.

I was sitting in an airport all checked in and waiting for my flight number to call for boarding. Travelling has always been one of my first love and I have travelled far and wide.

One thing that always strikes me when travelling is that once you are in the terminal you are surrounded by people of every kind, skin tones, languages, postures, and stories. You will witness something sacred, the fingerprint of God on diversity, yet this something many of us miss. We often miss the divine in the ordinary; but moments like these remind me that God is an artist and his favorite canvas is humanity.

We were not meant to be the same and yet, our hearts beat with the same borrowed breath. Our minds, though shaped by different cultures, all crave for truth, love and belonging. Heaven will not be dull, it will be a chorus of colors, cultures and languages all harmonizing one anthem worthy is the Lamb.

Let us think about it, in a world divided by differences, the church must model unity with diversity. Not erasing what makes us distinct but celebrating it as we pursue the same eternal destination.

Reflection

Let us all ask ourselves these questions: Am I actively celebrating the differences in others, or am I quietly resisting what makes people unlike me?

Is my life truly aligned with the path of Christ or am I just sitting in the terminal, assuming I am headed in the right direction?

Prayer

Dear God of all people, though we come from different paths, shape us into one family of grace. Help us honor every face we meet, seeing Your image in each person.
Guide our steps toward the same destination, a life rooted in love, justice, and compassion.
In Jesus name Amen.

Chapter 42

The Unity of Our Journey

Part Two

John 14:6 (NIV)
"Jesus said to him, I am the way, and the truth, and the life. No one comes to the Father except through me".

Different roads may shape us but only one Way can save us.

Though many flights were departing from the airport, all of us seated in that terminal lounge were all headed to one destination, JFK airport in New York. When I think back, I thought of that scene as a comparison of life under Christ. We come from various places, spiritual histories and personal struggles, but there is one Savior and one path that leads to the Father.

Though we live in a world that promotes tolerance without telling the truth and difference without giving direction; yet the gospel is completely inclusive because everyone is invited, and yet, it is also unapologetically exclusive as Jesus is the only way.

The beauty of our unity is not in sameness but in alignment. Not in always agreeing but in surrendering to the same King. In the body of

Christ, we can sit next to someone utterly different from us and still call them brother or sister, not because we look alike but because we walk the same road of grace.

Reflection

Am I actively celebrating the differences in others, or am I quietly resisting what makes people unlike me?

Is my life truly aligned with the path of Christ or am I just sitting in the terminal, assuming I am headed in the right direction?

Prayer

Father, thank You for the breathtaking beauty in Your creation especially in people. Forgive me for the times I have allowed my comfort to outweigh my compassion, or my opinions to outshout Your truth is what unite us, Lord, not just in mission but in spirit. Teach me to love as You love, beyond differences and despite disagreements. Above all keep me on the path that leads to You Jesus, as you are the only Way, the only Truth, the only Life. In Jesus name Amen.

Chapter 43

Fruitful and Familiar

Part One - The Tree Had to Go

Matthew 7:16–17 (NIV)
"By their fruit you will recognize them. Do people pick grapes from thornbushes, or figs from thistles? Likewise, every good tree bears good fruit, but a bad tree bears bad fruit".

Some blessings grow so quietly into your life, you forget they are extraordinary until they are gone.

For over twenty years, I had this big mango tree at the front of my house. It was not just a tree it was part of the rhythm of my life. It gave shade to our family, and it gave shelter with birds singing in it.

Lizards found refuge and twice a year it showed off its branches bending under the weight of big, sweet mangoes, hanging almost to the ground. It did not miss a season and it never forgot to bless us.

People came from everywhere, some asked permission to pick, others just took the mangoes as it did not matter because the tree had enough to give. It was known and it was loved and it was mine.

I remember one of my neighbor once said during one of those mango-heavy years, "It is not the tree that is blessed it is you, the tree is just carrying some of your blessings." That stayed with me because he was right. That tree was not just fruitful it was a symbol of the goodness in my life. The overflow, the grace, the favor and the kind of quiet abundance that becomes so familiar you may forget to marvel at it.

Yet that is what happens sometimes, is it not? We get used to what once amazed us, we forget to see the sacred in what is ordinary until change comes knocking.

On this first day before we talk about loss or hard decisions I want to pause and remember the fruit. To honor the seasons when the blessings were undeniable and the ground was generous because gratitude is not just for what we gain it is also the anchor we hold when it is time to let go.

Reflection

What parts of your life have become so familiar that you have stopped recognizing them as blessings?

Is there a fruitful tree in your life, a season, person or place that once overflowed with grace and still deserves your gratitude?

Prayer

Lord, thank You for the seasons of abundance. For the trees in my life that bore fruit for shade, shelter, sweetness and joy. Forgive me for the times I took familiar blessings for granted. Help me to pause and remember not with regret but with reverence. Let me carry gratitude like fruit in my hands, even when the branches are bare. In Jesus name Amen.

Chapter 44

The Root of the Matter.

Part 2

Ecclesiastes 3:1–2 (NIV)
"There is a time for everything, and a season for every activity under the heavens: a time to be born and a time to die, a time to plant and a time to uproot".

Some things you love must be removed not because they stopped bearing fruit, but because they have started threatening your foundation.

We did not see it at first because for years the mango tree was nothing but a gift standing big and tall at the front fence. Each year it was laden with big mangoes feeding people, bringing joy and marking seasons. It was part of the landscape and part of our lives.

Recently we noticed something disturbing, the roots were spreading and they were inches from going under the foundation of the house. That changed everything because now it did not matter how fruitful the tree was. It did not matter how many people loved it, it did not matter how beautiful or familiar or special it had become.

The roots were threatening what held the house together, and in that moment, I had to make a hard decision; would it be the mangoes or the foundation and I chose the foundation.

It was not easy because people gathered and neighbors came to watch. Some shared stories and others just looked on with silent mourning, almost as if something holy was being taken down. I smiled politely, kept my best face but deep down it hurt because it was not just the end of a tree, it was the end of a season.

After some time, here is what I am learning, love does not always mean holding on, sometimes love is choosing what will last over what was lovely. Even good things, beautiful, fruitful and blessed things can become dangerous when they start pushing into places they were never meant to reach. When they do, it takes wisdom to say: "You were a blessing but now it is time to let go."

Reflection

Is there anything in your life that was once fruitful, but now threatens your emotional, spiritual or relational foundation?

Are you holding onto something out of sentiment that God is gently asking you to release for the sake of long-term stability?

Prayer

Dear God, please give me the strength to make the hard decisions even when they cost me something precious. Help me discern what's blessing me from what's threatening me. I do not want to hold onto anything that puts my foundation at risk. Give me peace in letting go, and the faith to trust that You are making room for something new. In Jesus name Amen.

Chapter 45

What's Left Behind

From The Tree Had to Go

Ecclesiastes 3:3 (NIV)
"A time to kill and a time to heal, a time to tear down and a time to build."

When something beautiful is taken away, God uses the space to grow new blessings sometimes not just for you, but for those around you too.

The men sawed through the trunk and the truck came and hauled away the great mango tree. All that remained was an empty space and a hollow hole where fruit, shade and life once thrived.

I stood there feeling the ache of loss and the silence of a presence that was now gone. Then something unexpected happened, two neighbors came over asking if they could get some work done. "Can we get the men to cut down some trees in our yards too?" they asked joking about making them do a full day of work.

It struck me then that even in the emptiness, my letting go was making room for something new. My obedience became someone else's opportunity and my loss was a spark for their gain. There is a strange and beautiful grace in that.

Think about this, when we release what we can no longer keep then we don't just clear space for ourselves, but we even clear space for community, for new stories and for unexpected blessings.

That empty space in front of my house is no longer just a loss; it's a starting point and an invitation to trust that God is always at work. He is building, growing, blessing even when the fruit has fallen.

Reflection

What spaces in your life have been emptied by loss or change and how might God be inviting new growth there?

How can your experience of letting go become a blessing or encouragement to someone else?

Prayer

Father Lord, thank You for making space in my life when things must end. Help me see beyond the loss to the new life You are growing. Use my empty places to bless others and remind me that Your plans are always for renewal. Give me courage to trust in Your timing and peace in the waiting. In Jesus name Amen.

Chapter 46

When the Strong Hands Grow Still

Isaiah 40:7–8 (NIV)
"The grass withers and the flowers fall, because the breath of the Lord blows on them. Surely the people are grass. The grass withers and the flowers fall, but the word of our God endures forever."

We are not promised permanence only presence, and presence is enough, if we carry it with love.

This chapter is a tribute to Mr. Vernon (my neighbor) and every hand that gave quietly, every heart that aged gently and every presence that still lives in the spaces that we pass by.

I moved to that city nearly twenty years ago and at the time, I didn't know much then, new city and new rhythms but I found something steady in my neighbor Mr. Vernon. He was the kind of man who was like a community; if there was a broken pipe he would fix it, or a storm coming he would pull down the awning before you even asked. When a door lock jammed it would be just a call across the fence and he was there, tools in hand, always willing and never loud about it.

I brought him small gifts from my travels, and he never wanted to take them. "Miss B," he would say, "you are too good to me." This week I went home and Mr. V did not come to the fence.

I called his wife while I was holding his usual gift in my hand. She met me with eyes full of long quiet grief. "I can take it, for him, it does not make sense to come inside because he will not recognize you as he no longer talks." Something in me paused not just my body but in my soul just thinking of how she stood there, she looked like about seventy years old grieving the slow, cruel goodbye of someone she had loved since they were eighteen.

There I was, holding a small gift that he would never open and telling stories he would never hear again about the time he watched over my house while I was abroad and how he noticed people stealing mangoes from my tree and how he always stood guard even when no one saw.

Yet now he does not know, and he cannot hear and he will not remember and that is when the truth settled in, that even the strongest hands grow still; even the familiar voices grow quiet and even the things we do every day will become memories.

Yet when I think about love? Love does not vanish because it folds itself into the air, into fences and stories, and storm-prepped awnings and broken pipes that get fixed without a word. Love is shown in the ways we keep showing up with a gift in hand even when it will not be opened.

We are not promised endless time here, but we are promised presence. God's presence and the presence of people like Mr. V, who teach us how to love simply, consistently and quietly until their hands can no longer do what their hearts can do.

Reflection

Who are the quiet "Mr. V's" in your life those who served, showed up and held space for you in ways words could never repay?

How are you being called to honor presence over permanence to give, to love, to show up, even when it may not be remembered?

Prayer

Lord, thank You for the steady souls who cross our paths and make life feel held. Thank You for the hands that helped us, and for the kindness that never asked for credit. Teach me to honor them in memory and in action, and when the strong hands grow still, let mine carry the legacy forward. In Jesus name Amen.

Chapter 47

Still at the Fence: **When the Strong Hands Grow Still.**

Corinthians 13:7–8
"Love bears all things, believes all things, hopes all things, endures all things. Love never fails".

There is a quiet kind of love that doesn't leave, it just stands at the fence and holds the memory.

This chapter is a tribute to Mr. Vernon my neighbor's wife, and to every soul who loves through fading seasons. It is also a gentle reminder that not all ministries happen in churches, sometimes it happens at fences, in kitchens. at hospital bedsides and in soft aching silences.

She came to the fence when I called but she did not look like her usual self. She looked slimmer and not with her usual warmth but with a weight in her eyes. The kind of weight you carry when you have loved someone for more than fifty years, and now they no longer recognize your face.

I was holding a package with something small for Mr. V, just like I always brought when I visited. But her words froze the moment: I can take it, but it doesn't make sense to come inside.

He won't recognize you because he no longer talks, then She cried, seventy years old and together with him since she was eighteen. They had built an entire life together, shared storms, laughter, long nights, inside jokes and Sunday mornings.

Now she stands at the fence alone, he is still breathing but fading. He is still here but no longer home in himself and yet she stays, she bears it, she listens and she loves. Not with fireworks or grand gestures but with her presence, with consistency and with grief, that knows its place but doesn't ask for a stage.

It hit me then that there are so many kinds of strength, but the strength of a woman who still shows up even when the love she once had no longer speaks her name, that is a strength heaven recognizes. She is not waiting for thanks, she is not clinging to what was, but she is honoring what still is.

Why is she doing that, because love, real love, doesn't run when the lights dim, but it stays. It holds hands through the silence, it stands at the fence, holding memory like a fragile gift, retelling stories to anyone who will listen and sometimes, just to God. That is more than relationships, it is more than marriage, that is holy.

Reflection

Have you ever witnessed or lived the kind of love that keeps showing up, even when nothing comes back in return?

What does faithful presence look like in your season and who needs you to simply stand at the fence?

Prayer

Father, Thank You for the women who stay. For those who love in silence. For those who carry decades of memory with no audience. Bless their strength not the kind that roars, but the kind that endures. When words are gone, let love remain. When recognition fades, let honor rise. And when the world forgets, let heaven record every quiet act of faithfulness. In Jesus name Amen.

Chapter 48

The Ones Who Didn't Call Back

Psalm 118:8 (KJV)
"It is better to trust in the LORD than to put confidence in man"

Sometimes the ones you thought would show up don't and the ones you barely knew come carrying grace.

My daughter was pregnant with her first child and I wanted to be near her to walk with her through the last stretch of her pregnancy. So, she came to stay with me, we laughed, waited, hoped. We drove to the clinic, we read the reports, and we talked about the baby. Her husband was far away, but his conversations remained constant across the miles.

We lived on the fourth floor and then one morning, we went downstairs and saw a sign at the bottom of the stairs. "This building is no longer safe. Repairs must be completed by the date listed." The elevator was out of service with no warning and no explanation. Panic had set in, questions more than answers; how would my daughter heavily pregnant climb those stairs? What if we had to move quickly? What if something went wrong?

So, I did what anyone would do, I called my friends and I called people I trusted to be there for us. People who in other seasons, I had shown up for; yet after many calls, no one had a place and many called back a day or two later to check in, asking if we were alright.

One person who I believed was a true friend, never responded. There did not call, there were no check-ins, no apology and no form of explanation. Even now when my grandson is three years old and that moment from three years past remains unspoken, no words ever came.

Then someone I knew who was more of an acquaintance than a friend, volunteered to take us in. There was no hesitation, and we did not even have to ask the question. This was pure generosity, yet before I accepted the Holy Spirit nudged me: "Go to the City Office. Get the details for yourself." I went and the truth shifted everything.

The City Office explained that a step on one of the staircases was cracked. The elevator was not condemned, just out of service awaiting a part to repair it; and by law, it couldn't stay down for long without being repaired. We were safe and we didn't need to move and just like that, peace returned.

What stayed with me was not just fear or the sign or even safety. It was the silence of the one friend I thought would surely check in, who never did. It was about the grace that the another gave, who was ready to open their door without being asked.

Sometimes life teaches us not to place all our weight in human hands; even the good ones and even well-meaning ones. Not because they don't care but because God is our refuge and when He sees us vulnerable, He doesn't always use the people we expect; but He always sends someone and that's enough.

Reflection

Have you ever felt abandoned or overlooked in a moment when you needed help the most?

How have you seen God show up for you through unexpected people or paths?

Prayer

Lord, Thank You for being my true refuge, the One who never forgets me in crisis. Help me release the pain of disappointment when others don't show up. Help me see Your hand, even in the unexpected responses of strangers. Teach me to forgive without needing closure and to extend the same grace I have received. Let my trust rest in You first and everyone else second. In Jesus name Amen.

Chapter 49

The Panic, the Sign and the Silence

Psalm 146:3 (KJV)

"Put not your trust in princes, nor in the son of man, in whom there is no help".

Nothing humbles the heart like needing help and finding silence where you expected comfort.

For hours after returning home I sat with several "what ifs" still tugging at my heart. What if we had to get to the hospital quickly? What if labor started?

Suddenly the walls felt closer and the air felt tighter. I picked up my phone and started calling everyone I had called before to give them the change in circumstances. Yet my mind was still on the people who had once said, "Let me know if you ever need anything." I was still thinking that I wasn't asking for luxury but just a temporary place to stay while we figured things out.

Some called back later, some checked in the next day but that one friend, someone I thought was a real friend never responded at all, not even with a text or with a "sorry I can't help." I had expected to hear a "how are you holding up?", but somehow that silence hurt more than anything else.

Here is the truth, when you are vulnerable and are already stretched thin, the absence of someone you counted on feels heavier than the crisis itself and I didn't know what to do with that silence. I didn't know how to name it without sounding ungrateful or petty. The silence felt like a sting, and I felt that sting for a long time.

Reflection

Have you ever reached out in a moment of real need and been met with silence from someone you trusted?

How did that experience shape your view of friendship, boundaries, or God's faithfulness?

Prayer

Father, I know people are human and they forget, they miss things, they have their own battles. But it still hurts when the ones I hoped would show up don't. Give me space to feel the weight of disappointment without becoming bitter. Help me bring that silence to You and not to hold anyone responsible for anything that they have done but to take it to you. In Jesus name Amen.

Chapter 50

When the Hill Reminds Me

Psalm 37:23–24 (NIV)
"The Lord makes firm the steps of the one who delights in Him; though he may stumble, he will not fall, for the Lord upholds him with His hand."

God does not rush us on the road instead He walks with us, steadying every mile we fear to take.

A friend once told me about an unforgettable encounter she had while living in Upstate New York. One morning, someone at her workplace didn't show up, and she was asked to fill in at the warehouse. The only challenge was that the warehouse could only be reached by travelling on a route that made the vehicle feel like it was about to flip upside down because there was a steep hill with sharp corners and a deep drop-off that made your stomach twist.

She started the journey, but halfway along the road she felt overwhelmed. Fear gripped her as she crawled along at barely ten miles per hour. The road felt too high, too narrow and too dangerous. Her heart raced while her car crept almost not moving.

Suddenly, she heard a loud siren behind her, the traffic had built up because no one could pass. A police officer finally reached her window and asked if she was okay. Gently but firmly, he told her she had to go faster because she was holding up all the other vehicles. Breathless, she told him, "I can't, I'm too afraid to go any faster because I don't know what will happen."

What she didn't realize, though, was that she was near the end of the journey, the warehouse she feared she might never reach was just about a mile ahead. Fear had blinded her from seeing how close she was to her destination. She was almost there but the pressure, the anxiety and the steep climb made it impossible to recognize how near victory truly was.

Isn't that just like us? Sometimes the road feels too steep, the corners too sharp and the climb too much. We move slowly, unsure, scared of what might happen if we keep going. Yet God gently reminds us that He is there not behind us shouting, but beside us guiding.

The road may be frightening, and the journey may feel long, but sometimes the place God is leading us is only a mile ahead even when it looks impossible.

And just like that officer came alongside her, God walks with us, whispering courage into fear-filled places, reminding us that we are closer than we think.

Don't stop on the steep road. Don't quit at the bend. You may be nearer than you realize to the place God has been leading you. Keep moving maybe one mile, one moment and even one breath at a time. God will steady your hands, strengthen your heart and carry you forward.

Reflection

Where do I feel "stuck on the road," and how might God be calling me to continue despite fear?

What signs of God's presence can I recognize beside me as I journey forward?

Prayer

Lord, give me strength when the road is steep and courage when fear slows me down. Walk with me around every sharp corner and lift my eyes to see how close Your promises truly are. Keep me moving, trusting, and leaning on You. In Jesus name Amen

Chapter 51

Sometimes they are Messengers

Luke 12:6 (KJV)
"Are not five sparrows sold for two pennies? Yet not one of them is forgotten by God".

Heaven does not always speak in thunder, sometimes it visits on wings, waits in silence and leaves behind a whisper you only hear when you slow down enough to remember.

After the passing of the Covid 19 pandemic, I took a job working from home. Most days there are routine emails, meetings, screens but my desk faces the balcony, and sometimes the view becomes my sanctuary.

That day, something different happened. Three birds came; one dark with black-feathered and perched on the top rail looking distant and still. The other two had a soft blue and gray color, like sparrows and fluttered gently among the plants, as if exploring, as if whispering to each other in bird-language I could not understand.

Then the black one flew away and the two stayed, long enough for me to grab my phone, take pictures and record a video. They moved like they belonged there, like they had come on purpose. Exactly one month later and to the day they came again. The same two but not the black bird this time. It was just the pair of sparrows, glancing up now and then as if they were checking on me.

I didn't think much of it back then, I was in a hard place spiritually and emotionally worn. I was tired, pushing through and too buried in work to reflect. Yet looking back now I wonder, were they messengers? Did I miss the message because I was too caught up in the noise to listen?

Or maybe, God wasn't waiting on me to respond right then, maybe He just wanted me to see, to remember later, to recognize that in my exhaustion, I was still being watched over.

The thing about messengers is they don't always come when we are listening, they come when God sends them and sometimes the message is this, that it is stunningly sacred, not loud and not dramatic but in just a whisper on the wings of birds and you noticed.

Sometimes God doesn't use thunder, he uses sparrows and the fact that I remembered it months later, while reflecting on the season I was in tells me that I did not miss the message, I just had not unwrapped it yet.

Reflection

How often do I overlook the "sparrows" in my life the small, ordinary moments through which God may be sending a quiet message of comfort, direction, or reassurance?

What simple signs or gentle nudges has God placed around me recently that I might have dismissed because I was expecting something louder, bigger, or more dramatic?

Prayer

Lord, open my eyes to the small messengers You send my way. Teach me not to overlook the gentle signs of Your presence. Help me hear Your voice in the simple, the quiet, and the ordinary just as You care for the sparrows, remind me that You are always caring for me. In Jesus name Amen.

Chapter 52

The Dunns River Experience

Mark 4:39–40 (NIV)
"He got up, rebuked the wind and said to the waves, 'Quiet! Be still!' Then the wind died down and it was completely calm. He said to His disciples, 'Why are you so afraid? Do you still have no faith?'"

Faith does not make the waters still; it reminds us that Jesus is still in the boat.

Years ago we took a trip to Dunn's River, a famous place in Jamaica where the river meets the sea and the waterfalls pound your back like a lesson in endurance. The cascading water felt like strength, renewal, and refreshment, but surprisingly that wasn't the moment that stayed with me. The highlight was something much less predictable.

At one point during the trip, everyone decided to take a boat ride to explore the deeper parts of the water and knowing me I was ready. It would be adventure first and questions later. We all climbed aboard the boat with two boatmen, eager to look down at the sea floor through the glass bottom and take pictures of everything around us.

Then halfway out I heard one of the boatmen shout, "Everyone please put on your life jackets, we are having an engine failure." In that moment, my heart seemed to jump into my throat. People scrambled for life jackets, pulling them close and fastening them on. But instead of putting one on, I screamed, panicked and cried out, "I can't swim!" No one could calm me because fear took over completely.

Thankfully, after a few attempts, the engine coughed back to life, and the boat steadied once again. We continued our sightseeing as if nothing had happened, but I knew something inside me had shifted.

Whenever I look back on that day, I can't help but think of the disciples. They too were in a boat, facing waters they could not control, crying out in fear even with Jesus right there. Just like me, they forgot for a moment who was in charge of the wind, the waves and everything in between.

The river reminded me that fear doesn't make you weak; it makes you human but calling on Jesus in the middle of that fear, that is what makes you strong.

The same God who calmed the storm for the disciples is the same God who keeps our boat steady when life feels like it is breaking down beneath us. He doesn't always stop the fear instantly, but He never leaves the boat and He always gets us safely to shore.

Wherever your life feels unsteady today, just call on Jesus. Don't let panic drown out His presence. Remember that storms reveal the strength of the One who sails with you. Trust Him, breathe and hold on because the God of the river is also the God of your rescue.

Reflection

Where do I feel like the "engine has failed" in my life, and how is God inviting me to trust Him in that moment?

How do I usually respond to fear and how can I invite Jesus into that response?

Prayer

Lord, when the waters rise and fear grips my heart, remind me that You are in the boat with me. Calm my mind, steady my steps, and strengthen my faith. Help me to trust Your presence more than I fear the storm. In Jesus name Amen.

Chapter 53

God Speaks Through the Leaves

Psalm 46:10 (KJV)
"Be still, and know that I am God: I will be exalted among the heathen, I will be exalted in the earth".

When the soul is quiet, the trees start talking and the breeze brings messages only the spirit can hear.

In a previous chapter we read the somber story of when the birds came. Sometimes we say, "God does not speak to me like that, but what if He has been speaking all along and we have just been too busy, too tired, too distracted to recognize his voice when it does not sound like words?

After the sparrows visited my balcony not once, but twice I began to realize something: God had been speaking to me, not with thunder, but with subtleness, with birds, with silence and even with the way the light touched the plants at 10 a.m. Sometimes even with the stillness between tasks and with the pause before a decision.

He was in the in-between, but I was always rushing past it. I had been looking for signs in solutions, for confirmation in outcomes, for help in the people I expected it from.

Instead, He sent sparrows, he sent a breeze, he sent a moment that would only make sense in reflection. God doesn't force anything; he doesn't demand your attention. He just is God, and if you are still enough, he reveals what has been showing you all along:

Sometimes God's fingerprints, his messages, his presence may be your invitation to put down the phone. To pause the schedule. To sit on the balcony or the porch or beside a window. and just listen. Not for words, but for presence. For the language of wind, the sermon in the birdsong, the scripture being written in the shade of trees.

He still speaks, he hasn't stopped and when our souls grow quiet enough, we begin to remember the sound of His voice.

Reflection

What does "being still" look like in your life right now?

Can you recall a time when something in nature a bird, tree, breeze, or sunset felt like a message directly to your spirit?

Prayer

Dear God, You speak in thunder and in whispers You are in the wind and the stillness. Help me tune my ears again to the sound of

You. Unclutter my soul, still my racing thoughts and help me fall in love again with the simplicity of being with You in quiet places, among quiet things, where You are always waiting. In Jesus name Amen.

Chapter 54

When the Voice Goes Silent

Part One: The Room I Almost Didn't Enter

Amos 8:11 (NIV)

The days are coming, declares the Sovereign Lord, when I will send a famine through the land not a famine of food or a thirst for water, but a famine of hearing the words of the Lord".

Sometimes the loudest silence comes after the most spiritual noise.

It was a Saturday morning during the thick of the Covid-19 pandemic. I had just finished a virtual counseling session with a client when a text came in from my prayer partner: "I think you should join us in this Zoom room. it's a prophetic service."

Honestly? I almost hissed my teeth, I wasn't interested and I didn't know these people, so I didn't want anyone "speaking over my life" when I hadn't even discerned their spirit. Fifteen minutes later, she texted again, "Come in now."

I don't know why I did, maybe out of curiosity, maybe out of loyalty, but I clicked the link and entered the Zoom room. Not long after I joined, the prophet someone I had never met, called my name and I almost froze.

He began to speak over me, releasing what he called "words from the Lord." Some of what he said hit deep, because they were specific and personal things he should not have known, but other parts made me pause and ponder. Some things did not sit right in my spirit, and I could not explain why. Still, I continued joining the online services week after week.

Then something shifted, the flow I once had with God started to dry up. My dreams became still, my prayer time felt empty and it was as if heaven went quiet. I kept going to the meetings, I kept listening but inside it felt like a desert, like what scripture described when the word of the Lord became rare.

Was this a test? Had I stepped into something out of alignment? Was God offended? Was I off track? Or was this just a necessary silence, the kind that forces you to go deeper, lower and further?

I don't know when it happened exactly, but one day I looked up and realized that I was still in church, but I was not in communion. The voice of God once close, near and daily was quiet and no one tells you how disorienting that silence can be.

Reflection

Have you ever walked through a season where you were showing up to church or spiritual spaces, but still felt distant from God?

How do you usually respond when God feels silent do you press in, pull back or try to fill the silence with other voices?

Prayer

Lord, Your silence speaks, but I confess sometimes I don't know how to hear it. I miss Your voice. I miss the nearness I once felt. If I have stepped out of alignment, draw me back. If I am in a wilderness, walk with me through it and if You are simply teaching me to listen differently, please give me the humility to receive Your lessons in silence. In Jesus name Amen.

Chapter 55

When the Silence Breaks

Part Two
Jeremiah 29:12–13
"Then shall ye call upon me, and ye shall go and pray unto me, and I will hearken unto you. And ye shall seek me, and find me, when ye shall search for me with all your heart".

God's silence is never absence it is an invitation and when you come closer, He speaks again.

I had stayed in the space for months, still showing up to the prophetic zooms and still keeping my spiritual routines, but inside I was dry. It felt like I had traded intimacy for information and there were voices in meetings but no whisper from God.

Eventually I had to be honest with myself, I missed God not the gatherings, not the prophetic words but Him. So, I made a choice and I pulled back. I stopped attending the services that once felt powerful. It was not in bitterness but in hunger, I knew what I was missing and I wanted it back.

So, I returned to the basics of deliberate fasting, intentional prayer, quiet spaces and sacred seeking. To the place where there were no screens and no prophetic meetings, no background noise but just me, my Bible, my worship, and a heart that said:

"Lord, I don't want a word about You I want to hear from You again." Then slowly it began to happen, a dream here, a vision there then the clear unmistakable moments where God began to speak again. It was not through someone else's voice but through my own spirit, through scripture, through quiet impressions, trough the secret sacred language I had always known with Him.

And I cried and cried, not just because He spoke but because I realized that he had never stopped loving me. He had never truly left, he was simply inviting me to come closer than I ever had before and then I did.

The silence wasn't punishment, it was pulling me deeper and quieter, back to the place where his voice matters more than anyone else's. I am still on that journey, still learning continue to fast, to listen, to wait but now I know something I didn't have before.

None of us can live off borrowed fire, you can't sustain your spirit on secondhand revelations because the presence of God must be personal or it will never be enough.

Reflection

What do you think God might be inviting you to lay down so you can come closer to Him again?

Have you ever had to choose between familiar spiritual comfort and a deeper, more personal pursuit of God?

Prayer

Lord, Thank You for trusting me with silence. Thank You for not speaking when You knew I needed to seek You for myself. Thank You for drawing me back, not with fear, but with longing. I cherish Your voice. I crave Your presence. I commit to pursuing You not just through people or platforms, but in the secret place You have prepared just for You and me. Speak again, Lord. I am listening In Jesus name Amen.

Remember if God is silent, the silence is never the end. It is the doorway and if you seek, fast and wait will find the key. He still speaks and now and you will know the sound of His voice again.

Chapter 56

Even The Trees Can Remind Me

Psalm 23:2-3 (NIV)
"He makes me lie down in green pastures, he leads me beside quiet waters, he refreshes my soul. He guides me along the right paths for his name's sake".

Sometimes it is not the absence of noise but the presence of peace that tells me where I truly belong.

There was something sacred about my old home, the trees stood tall and green, alive with life. The birds made music on my balcony as if they knew I needed their song. That balcony became a holy invitation warm, always calling me to sit with my tea, to breathe, to be still and just to be.

Then there was my closet; it wasn't just for clothes it was my prayer closet, my meeting place with God. A sacred rhythm I didn't realize had become the anchor of my peace.

Then I left, not recklessly but with reason as there was a better job, a new opportunity, more income and a move that made sense on paper. Yet something left me in the process, as I stepped into the new and slowly the quiet faded. The meditation dwindled and the prayer closet disappeared into busyness.

I didn't realize how empty I had become until I returned home one weekend and the green trees whispered what my soul had then forgotten. As if to say, "You were never meant to survive without stillness." That's when I came to myself.

Reflection

What sacred rhythms have I let slip away in this season?

Have I mistaken provision for peace and is God calling me back to both?

Prayer

Father, bring me back to the places where my soul breathes. Help me to see that success without stillness is not Your design. Restore to me the rhythms that drew me close to You, the trees, the silence, the song, the prayer. Don't just prosper my hands keep my heart in peace. In Jesus name Amen.

Chapter 57

The Place Where I Came to Myself

Part 2: When the Trees Remind Me

Luke 15:17 (KJV)
"And when he came to himself, he said, How many hired servants of my father's have bread enough and to spare, and I perish with hunger"!

The moment we come to ourselves is often the moment we begin returning to God.

I didn't see it right away. I told myself I was doing the right thing, taking care of responsibilities, honoring the opportunity and being wise. Yet over time I began to feel something missing.

It was not just the birds or the trees or the physical space it was the presence I had lost but it was also the stillness and the grounding. The daily touchpoints with God that had once carried me through and then I went home, not just physically but spiritually.

For one weekend, I walked into the familiar and there, surrounded by everything I had unknowingly starved myself of, I heard that sacred whisper: "You are trying to do your best, but not at the right time."

That moment reminded me of the prodigal son not because I had rebelled, but because I had drifted, I was still working, still serving, still pressing forward but I had wandered from peace and like him, I came to myself and in that, I started my return to sacred rhythm to rest and to God.

Reflection

Let this be more than a reflection, let it be your return. You are not behind you are just being called back and there is still peace waiting for you.

Chapter 58

Even the Trees can Remind You

Psalm 23:2-3 (KJV)
"He maketh me to lie down in green pastures: he leadeth me beside the still waters. He restoreth my soul: he leadeth me in the paths of righteousness for his name's sake".

Sometimes it is not the absence of noise but the presence of peace that tells you where you truly belong.

As discussed in the past two chapters, I had to make way for a part three writing specifically to you. Think about it, in your former home or even life in your earlier days, the green trees, the singing birds, the quiet balcony, and even the sacred stillness of your prayer closet may have formed a kind of sanctuary not just in structure, but in your soul.

These were not mere luxuries; they were lifelines. Sacred rhythms that joined you to your Creator. Yet in pursuit of more, you may have traded the eternal for the external. It's easy to assume that elevation in status means alignment with God's will but even the highest mountain can feel empty if God's peace is not dwelling with you there.

Sometimes we do not realize how far we have drifted until we return to the waters that once restored us and there amidst the leaves, the light and the silence we come back to ourselves and to God.

Remember: Let this be more than a reflection let it be your return. You are not behind you are just being called back and there is still peace waiting for you.

Reflection

What sacred rhythms have you let slip away in your current environment?

Have you mistaken provision for peace and is God calling you back to both?

Prayer

Father, remind me of what truly matters. When I chase what glitters, let the stillness of Your presence call me back. Bring me to the green pastures of Your will, where my soul is watered again. Help me not only to succeed — but to remain, rooted and full of peace. In Jesus name Amen.

Chapter 59

Purpose In The Waiting

Galatians 6:2 (NIV)
"Carry each other's burdens, and in this way you will fulfill the law of Christ."

Sometimes God whispers purpose through the quiet confessions of strangers, trusting me to hold what others can no longer carry alone.

There are moments in life when God does not speak through thunder, visions, or dreams but He speaks through people.

Lately, without invitation or prompting, hearts have been opening to me. Stories have been spilling out about childhood wounds, present battles, financial struggles and hidden fears. People I have known for years and people I have just met suddenly feel safe with me, drawn to share chapters of their lives they have kept closed from others.

I listen and sometimes I offer a few words of support, sometimes gentle advice, but most often I give what many are longing for which is encouragement, presence and a sense of being seen; because in those moments, I know God is at work.

One encounter in particular stays with me, a man who seemed close to homeless, worn and weary in appearance. Yet when he spoke, his humility softened every word. He told me about his life, his belongings, his struggles without defensiveness or pride. As I listened, something in me paused because I felt a sense of awe and not pity, purpose and not confusion.

I had to stop and ask, "Lord, is this You? Is this my calling unfolding right in front of me?" Sometimes we don't need to chase purpose because sometimes purpose chases us through the stories of others, through the pain they entrust to us, through the sacred honor of holding what they have carried alone for too long.

Discernment is not accidental and compassion is not incidental. Know that your presence is not random when people open up without hesitation, it is often a sign that God has marked us as a safe place, an earthly refuge for weary souls. While we may not fully understand it yet, we are walking in something divine.

Sometimes we are already in our calling long before we recognize it. Sometimes God places purpose in our hands before we even realize we are holding it. Sometimes the greatest ministries begin simply by listening.

Reflection

What emotions or spiritual nudges do I feel when people share their stories with me, and what might God be revealing through them?

How can I intentionally nurture this gift of listening and encouragement as a calling from God?

Prayer

Father, thank You for trusting me with the hearts and stories of others. Help me to listen with Your compassion, speak with Your wisdom, and love with Your grace. If this is the calling You've placed before me, reveal it clearly and guide me gently into it. Make me a safe place where Your presence can be felt through every interaction. In Jesus name Amen.

Chapter 60

Shelter in the Sudden

Part One: When the Rain Falls Without Warning

Psalm 46:1–2 (KJV)
"God is our refuge and strength, a very present help in trouble. Therefore will not we fear, though the earth be removed, and though the mountains be carried into the midst of the sea". **The rain may fall without warning but God never withholds the shelter.**

That morning I left the house like I have done many times before walking that familiar path, counting my steps, breathing in the rhythm of routine. The sky was overcast, but I have seen that before and did not expect anything out of the ordinary.

Then with no thunder to warn me it started to pour heavily, sudden heavy rain. Some people kept walking maybe thinking they could power through it but I ran for the trees. I knew the trees couldn't stop the rain from falling, but they could keep me from being overtaken by it.

That is how life is, one minute everything feels steady, predictable and safe. Then suddenly, you are caught in a storm emotionally, spiritually, financially and relationally. There was no warning and no build-up, just huge impact.

God does not always stop the storm, but he always makes sure we are not without shelter. Sometimes it is a person, sometimes it is a scripture, sometimes it is that holy silence under the tree of his presence. With God there is always a place to pause, to breathe, and to not be swallowed by what we did not see coming.

Reflection

What storms in your life came without warning and how did God provide shelter in that season?

Are you trying to press through a storm alone, when God might be inviting you to pause under His covering?

Prayer

Lord, thank You for being a present help not just a future hope. When storms come without warning, teach me to run to You first. You are my tree in the rain, my shelter in the sudden. Let me not be too proud to seek covering. Let me find peace even when the skies open up. In Jesus name Amen.

Chapter 61

After the Rain

Psalm 107:29–30 (NIV)
"He stilled the storm to a whisper; the waves of the sea were hushed. They were glad when it grew calm, and He guided them to their desired haven".

Every storm leaves a silence and in that silence God often speaks.

Eventually the rain let up, the heavy drops slowed to a drizzle and the trees dripping with what they had caught stood quiet again. I stepped back out and kept walking a little wetter, a little wiser and somehow more aware.

Storms don't cancel our journey; it did not for Jesus and his disciples. Storms only change our posture, I did not stop walking because of the rain, I waited in it and sometimes that is all God asks. Life will stary again, the sun will shine again, but it is never quite the same after the rain.

I have grown to learn what I can handle and what I can't handle without Him. I remember that even well-known paths can surprise me at times and I realize how much I still need daily grace, even when I think I know what the day holds. The path may be the same, but I am not,

I am storm-washed, soul-anchored and still walking.

Reflection

What did the last "storm" in your life teach you about yourself and about God?

How is God asking you to walk forward differently after the rain?

Prayer

Father, thank You for the rain and for the stillness that follows. Let me not just survive my storms but hear You in the silence they leave behind. Make me more tender, more trusting, and more attuned to Your presence, teach me to walk again, this time with more wisdom, more grace, and more You. In Jesus name Amen.

Chapter 62

God Leaves a Pen on the Floor

Philippians 4:19 (KJV)
"But my God shall supply all your need according to His riches in glory by Christ Jesus".

God's provision does not always arrive in the form we expect but it always comes right on time.

It was a simple morning, the kind that did not seem to hold anything special. Just a necessary errand: wash some linens, wait an hour, and not waste time while doing it.

So, I did what I usually do when I am trying not to waste the moment, I brought my Bible. This was not just any Bible, but my Bible, the one full of underlined verses, notes in the margins and prayers scribbled between the lines, always my companion in many quiet hours.

After loading the washers, I went back to the car ready to dive into the Word. Then I realized I had no pen. None was in my bag, the glove compartment or the car door pocket where there were always pens; no pen could be found.

To many people that might sound trivial but to those who read the Word not just with their eyes but with their whole heart, you may understand that the pen matters. The markings matter and they are part of how the Word becomes alive to me.

So, I sat there almost feeling frustrated and waiting while staring at the Bible I longed to relate with but could not in the way I was used to. Almost twenty-five minutes passed and still no reading, just waiting. Then came the thought, go check on the load in the washer and as I walked back into the laundromat just a few steps from the first machine I had used there it was, a pen lying on the floor, right in plain sight.

It stopped me in my tracks and my throat tightened. I bent down and picked it up gently, began to wipe it clean. Suddenly that pen was not just a pen it was provision, it was the presence of God.

I carried it back to the car with reverence and opened the Bible again, this time I did not just read the Word I underlined the words and felt the scriptures deeply.

God had reminded me that he sees every need, even the small ones, even the ones that feel too small to pray about and He provides not because he has to, but because He wants to. In that laundromat, God left me a pen on the floor.

It was not because I deserved it, but because He delights in showing up for His children.

Reflection

Is there something you have stopped praying for because it felt too small or not worth asking? God is not only the God of big miracles He is also the God of pens on the floor.

Today, bring your smallest needs to Him. Write them down. Speak them out, ask boldly, trust fully and watch how God provides not always how you expect but always when you need it.

Prayer

Father God, Thank You for caring about every detail of my life even the ones I think are too small for You. Help me to trust Your provision in the ordinary moments and to see Your hand in unexpected places. Thank You for the reminder that nothing escapes Your attention and that You are always nearby. Increase my faith in the little things and let me never forget that You are a faithful Provider. In Jesus' name In Jesus name Amen.

Chapter 63

When God Needs Your Attention

Psalm 46:10 (KJV)
"Be still and know that I am God: I will be exalted among the heathen, I will be exalted in the earth".

Sometimes God silences the noise not to deny us, but to draw us into a deeper awareness of His voice.

It was a quiet Tuesday morning and there was the kind of stillness that feels sacred. The clock read 5:30 AM as I sat in my car, parked outside on a simple errand. My usual rhythm on mornings like this was to plug into the church prayer line. the lifeline that had accompanied me faithfully for years.

With ready fingers, I dialed the same number, expecting to enter the prayer room seamlessly and into the spiritual presence of prayer and praise. Then something happened, a message came across the phone line and changed the routine I am used to. "This number is not included in your rate plan", the voice said decisively.

I blinked and was so confused, that had never happened before so I checked the number and tried again not once, but twice and the same decisive voice met me every time.

That is when the stillness around me shifted, it was not in fear but with a sense of awareness. What if God was speaking in the silence? What if this was not a disruption but an invitation to listen to him?

Suddenly, I remembered how often in Scripture, God interrupted normal patterns to get the attention of His people. Moses was tending to sheep when a burning bush refused to be consumed. Samuel was lying down when a voice called him by name. Elijah stood in a cave listening for God, but the voice was not in the wind or the fire or the earthquake, but it came in a whisper.

The moment I experienced was not about technology or telecommunication; I believe it was divinely orchestrated. God had something to say but not through the usual channel. He wanted me, my attention and alone and focused on him.

I believe the prayers of the church were still going on but God had scheduled a personal meeting with me which was not as part of a group, but a face-to-face and heart-to-heart meeting. I sat there with my phone resting on my lap and my eyes lifted to the sky. I did not have a script or a plan but I had a listening ear and a spirit that was ready to hear the words, be still, I am God.

In that stillness, I found a strange kind of peace and a powerful awareness that God still speaks outside the box we place Him in. He does not always come through the prayer line or the Sunday service or the favorite worship playlist. Sometimes, He comes in a blocked call, or a detour and even a divine pause and when He does, we must choose to listen.

Reflection

Has God been trying to get your attention lately, but you have been too busy with the routine of seeking Him to actually hear Him?

Take 10 minutes today to sit in silence, no phone and no music. Release yourself of every distraction and just say: "Speak, Lord, your servant is listening."

Prayer

Father God, Thank You for loving me enough to interrupt my routine. Help me to recognize when You are drawing me away to speak to me. Teach me to be still, to quiet the noise, and to listen for Your voice in unexpected places. I surrender my schedule, my expectations, and my methods to You. Speak, Lord I am listening. In Jesus' name, A In Jesus name men.

Chapter 64

The Bell Rings

Part One: A New Place a Familiar Sound

Matthew 24:42 (NIV)
"Therefore keep watch, because you do not know on what day your Lord will come."

Sometimes the smallest sound carries the loudest message if your heart is still enough to hear it.

Moving to a new area often brings a sense of disorientation. Gone are the familiar comforts, the trees that danced in the breeze, the birds that sing every morning, and the rhythms that shaped your days.

The new landscape is different with tall buildings lining the streets, standing shoulder to shoulder like silent sentinels. Nature seems absent, and so do the sounds that once whispered God's peace into your heart. Then something breaks through the silence: a bell.

Every morning at 7:00 a.m., it rings with a clear and unwavering sound in the middle of the city's stillness. At first, it was curious, then comforting and over time it became a part of my day, a rhythm in the unfamiliar. Yet, I wondered do others hear it too? Do they pause, even for a moment? Or has it faded into the background noise of daily life, unnoticed and unvalued?

I asked my family members if they hear the bell in the mornings and their response was "what bell". I explained to them and none of them have ever heard the bell. Just like that bell, God's presence often sounds quietly in our lives, not with clamor but with consistency.

Reflection

What distractions or commitments most often keep you from hearing God's voice, and what small change can you make today to give Him more of your attention?

When was the last time you intentionally slowed down to listen for God's guidance, and what did you sense Him speaking to your heart?

Prayer

Lord, quiet my mind and settle my spirit. Help me not to become so busy that I miss Your gentle voice. Teach me to pause, to listen, and to walk in step with You each day. Amen.

Chapter 65

Are We Listening?

Part Two

Matthew 24:42 (NIV)
"Therefore keep watch, because you do not know on what day your Lord will come."

The ringing of the bell remind me of something more eternal which is the coming of Christ.

Scripture tells us that He will return at a time that no one expects, and yet like the bell, there are signs and reminders all around us that gently nudges us calling us to be ready.

How many of us are truly listening? We live in a world filled with noise, distractions and deadlines and the sound of God's voice can seem like just another background frequency. Yet for those who are tuned in and for those who are watching, waiting and walking closely with Him it is a call to readiness.

The bell rings not only to mark time but to awaken the soul. It is a daily reminder to me that Christ is coming. Will we be prepared when He calls?

This week, find a moment each morning to pause and listen not just with your ears, but with your heart. Let the quiet be a space where God can speak.

Ask Him to heighten your spiritual sensitivity so that you won't miss His call, however softly it may come.

Reflection

What bells might God be ringing in your life to draw your attention to His presence or purpose?

In what ways can you practice spiritual attentiveness in your new surroundings, even when they feel unfamiliar or uncomfortable?

Prayer

Lord, quiet my mind and settle my spirit. Help me not to become so busy that I miss Your gentle voice. Teach me to pause, to listen, and to walk in step with You each day. In Jesus name Amen.

Chapter 66

Tending the Soul First

Part One: The Face Behind the Words

Proverbs 4:23
"Above all else, guard your heart, for everything you do flows from it."

What burdens the soul will eventually break the body unless we learn to care for what cannot be seen.

In our workplaces, which are more or less professional and structured, it is easy to focus on procedures, policies and solutions; but every so often, someone walks in who breaks through the routine.

This was a customer; not sure I saw her before. She looked tired not just physically, but emotionally as well. Her eyes told a story of battles fought in silence and her words came quickly, yet with weight: "I am drowning in debt, can you help me? Yet it was not just about the money, not really.

I recognized it, that expression was one of agony, despair and a kind of loneliness that sits heavy in the chest. It was familiar, not because I had seen it recently, but because I had once worn that heaviness myself at a point in my life. Her problem seemed financial, but what stood out to me first was the cry of her soul. That is where God directed my heart, it was not to her circumstance but to her person.

Reflection

How often do I pay attention not just to what people say, but to what their expressions and actions reveal about their true feelings or needs?

What might God be inviting me to notice in the "faces" around me those unspoken cues that call for compassion, patience, or deeper understanding?

Prayer

Lord, give me eyes to see beyond words and a heart sensitive to what others may be silently carrying. Help me reflect Your love by noticing, understanding, and responding with grace. In Jesus name Amen.

Chapter 67

The Ministry of Presence

1 Samuel 16:7 (NIV)
"The Lord does not look at the things people look at. People look at the outward appearance, but the Lord looks at the heart."

Sometimes the truth a person carries is written on their face long before it reaches their tongue, so listen with your eyes as well as your ears.

Jesus didn't always start with the problem people brought to Him. He saw beneath the symptoms into their hearts. When the woman at the well came for water, He offered her living water first. When others sought healing, He gave it before explaining the deeper truth, so that His ministry always touched the soul before addressing the surface.

So, I followed His lead and spoke. "Let us talk about why you came here today," I said. It was an invitation for her not just to speak, but to be seen. To be human again and not just another case to solve. Once the soul had room to breathe, the practical conversation about debt could follow but first she needed care not correction.

Before she left, I reminded her: "In everything, Judy, remember to take care of yourself." How many of us need that same reminder?

We run, we carry, we plan and we manage but forget to care for the one carrying it all which is ourselves. Not in a self-centered way, but in the way Scripture teaches. Guard your heart, care for your soul and tend to your spirit; because if the inside breaks, the outside eventually follows.

This week, slow down long enough to care for your own soul. Ask God to reveal the places within you that need tending, and when others come to you with their burdens, listen not just to the words, but to the heart behind them, minister presence before you give solutions.

Reflection

When was the last time you paused to care for your own soul not just your schedule, your work, or your responsibilities?

How can you begin offering soul-care to others before jumping into solving their surface problems?

Prayer

Lord, teach me to see others the way You see them not just their words, but their hearts. Help me notice the unspoken needs and respond with compassion, wisdom, and love.. Amen.

Chapter 68

Words Can Echo Back

Revelation 21:4 (NIV)
"He will wipe every tear from their eyes. There will be no more death or mourning or crying or pain, for the old order of things has passed away."

Our words can echo heaven even while we walk on earth.

A long-time friend recently reminded me of the quiet power carried in everyday speech. I have always admired how he never says goodbye. Instead, he would say, "Take care, see you soon," or "I will be back later," or "Catch you later." He closed every conversation with expectation and not with finality. He spoke hope instead of endings and continuity instead of closure.

His habit made me stop and think especially after hearing a song that declared goodbye to pain and sorrow. It made me wonder; Can we really say goodbye to pain and sorrow while we're still in this earthly form?

The truth is that pain and sorrow will visit every human soul. They come in seasons, waves or sometimes sudden storms. We feel them in our bodies, in our memories and in the quiet corners of our hearts.

Yet even in the middle of them God calls us to speak life. Scripture tells us that life and death are in the power of the tongue. Our words carry weight, direction, and spiritual resonance. They can tether us to despair, or they can pull us toward God's promises.

Maybe that is why my friend never says goodbye because in his own way, he refuses to speak finality where God has spoken continuity. Maybe he knows that even when seasons shift, God's faithfulness follows.

Let us think about this; what does God truly require of us? It is not that we should pretend pain is not real. Not that we deny the presence of sorrow. Rather, He calls us to anchor our words and our hearts in the world that is coming. A world where tears are wiped away and where grief cannot follow us. A world where pain is only a memory, not a companion.

We are living between two realities: the ache of now and the hope of what will be. Yet because of Christ, we are allowed to speak from the hope even while we stand in the ache. We can't yet say goodbye to every sorrow, but we *can* speak with the confidence that a day is coming when God Himself will close the final chapter of all suffering. On that day standing in the presence of perfect love we will finally be able to say goodbye.

Reflection

How do your daily words reflect the hope God promises, even when you are facing pain or sorrow?

What "goodbyes" are you longing for and how can you surrender them to God's future healing and restoration?

Prayer

Lord, teach me to use my words with Heaven in mind. Help me speak life, hope, and faith even in seasons of pain. Give me endurance for today and expectation for the day You wipe away every tear. In Jesus name Amen.

Chapter 69

Seeing the Heart

(1 Samuel 16:7, NIV)
"The Lord does not look at the things people look at. People look at the outward appearance, but the Lord looks at the heart."

Sight is a gift but seeing is a calling.

There is a kind of vision that goes far beyond the eyes. It is the quiet reading of the soul, that ability to hear someone's pain behind their silence, to sense their burdens behind their laughter and to read the untold chapter hiding behind their carefully chosen words.

Some years ago, I met a woman who never spoke a word to me at first. She simply stood there composed, polite and seemingly whole. Then in a single moment and without explanation, I saw her not with my eyes, but with the deeper awareness God sometimes breathes into us.

I felt the fractures in her story, the weight in her heart and the ache she hid behind her stillness. Then when she finally opened her mouth to speak, her words only confirmed what had already been revealed: her life had been carved by pain, but her spirit still fought for light.

Is this not what God invites His children to do? To see the heart the way He does beyond appearance, beyond presentation and beyond the surface that so often deceives us?

God's gaze has never been limited to the external. Scripture reminds us that from the heart flows the issues of life, joy, grief, hope, fear, wounds and worship. So, when we allow God to cultivate spiritual sight within us, we become His mirrors reflecting compassion where others offer criticism, discernment where others offer dismissal, and presence where others offer distance.

To see someone is a sacred act, to truly see them is an act of love; to respond as God does with tenderness, truth and grace is an act of obedience.

Reflection

When was the last time you looked beyond someone's behavior and asked God to show you their heart?

What distractions or assumptions keep you from seeing people the way God sees them?

Prayer

Father, open the eyes of my heart. Teach me to see people as You see them to notice their hidden hurts, their quiet needs, and their unspoken hopes. Give me compassion, discernment and the courage to respond with Your love. In Jesus name Amen.

Chapter 70

Joy Beyond Circumstances

Romans 10:8 (NIV)
"The word is near you; it is in your mouth and in your heart."

Sometimes the direction I need is only a breath away and God waits for me to speak so He can guide me to what He already prepared.

I usually take my lunch to work every day, not because I prefer to, but because the area where I work is filled with big stores and restaurants and the time, I am given for lunch just does not allow me to order, wait and then sit down to enjoy a hot meal. My home-cooked lunch is quick, simple and easy to reheat.

On this particular day, I did not bring lunch, and I did not even have breakfast. I stood there, trying to figure out what I was going to do as the hunger was real and time was short. It is interesting how sometimes all it takes is a comment or a question voiced out loud for a solution to present itself.

I was standing there with two teammates and without even thinking, I said, almost to myself, that I didn't have lunch and was not sure what I would do. One of them immediately responded, "Really? Why not go to the restaurant just three minutes down the road? They sell the best food, and you walk in and out in minutes with your takeaway".

You can imagine my delight not only did she name a place I would never consider, but she described exactly what I needed, quick and good food within reach. I went, got my meal in minutes, and was impressed with both the taste and the service.

Then it made me think, is not that what the Word of God is? It is near us, accessible, prepared and waiting and it is answers for our questions, guidance for our confusion and provision for our hunger both spiritual and emotional. Do we take the time to try it? Do we reach for it when we need direction? Do we speak up, pray, ask and seek so God can point us toward what has already been made ready for me?

If you are wondering, searching, or needing clarity, remember God's Word is right there closer than you think, quicker than you expect, and always nourishing to your soul. Sometimes all you need to do is open your mouth, express the need and allow Him to guide me.

Reflection

What situations in my life right now could be transformed if I intentionally turned to God's Word for direction?

How can I practice asking, seeking, and speaking to God more freely so I can receive the guidance He has already prepared for me?

Prayer

Lord, thank You for placing Your Word so close to me ready to guide, comfort, and feed my soul. Teach me to seek You first, to speak openly before You, and to trust that You have already prepared answers for my needs. Lead me to Your wisdom quickly, just as You lead me to provision when I least expect it. In Jesus name Amen.

Chapter 71

Mountains and Tunnels of Life

Psalm 121:1–2 (NIV)
"I lift up my eyes to the mountains—where does my help come from? My help comes from the Lord, the Maker of heaven and not earth."

God does not only guide our mountaintop moments; He steadies our steps in the dark tunnels that lead us there.

Part 1 The Tunnel

After years of accepting an invitation from a close friend to visit Spain, March of 2023 finally found me boarding a plane with two of my friends, full of anticipation and so unaware of how deeply the journey itself would speak to my heart.

From France to Málaga, and then to our final stop in Salobreña, the trip was rich with so much beauty, the sea, the breeze, the landscape and the peace. Yet there was something unexpected that caught my spirit and that was the tunnels.

On the drive from Málaga to Salobreña, we passed through tunnel after tunnel, they were so many I decided to take photos and start counting them. There were long ones, short ones, narrow ones and wide ones. Each tunnel briefly removed the view of the sea, the sunlight and sometimes the majestic mountains.

For a moment, everything was dark, then everything looked the same and felt even confined. Yet every single tunnel had one thing in common and that was an exit and what was further common is that light always greeted us on the other side.

Tunnels in life feel like those seasons when we can't see clearly, the times of waiting, of uncertainty, of transition or challenges. We don't always understand how long they will last and sometimes we fear we may never see light again. Yet tunnels are not ever our destination, they are only passageways. God does not leave us in them and He always leads us through them.

Even when you cannot see what is ahead, God is still driving the car. He sees the end from the beginning and the tunnel is not proof of His absence, but it is part of His guidance.

Stay purposeful as we continue with part two in the next chapter.

Reflection

Which season am I currently in, are you in a tunnel, season?

How is God inviting you to trust Him there?

Prayer

Lord, when I face the mountains of life, give me strength to climb. When I walk through the dark tunnels, give me light to guide my steps. Remind me that You are with me in every rise and every shadow, leading me toward hope, purpose, and peace. In Jesus name Amen.

Chapter 72

The Journey That Spoke

Part Two: The Mountains

As I continue on my journey from Malaga to Salobrena Spain, the second thing that captured my heart was the towering mountains and the valleys resting low at their feet. Some mountains stood high and bold, while others clustered together like great pillars reaching into the sky.

They reminded me of a simple truth we often forget and that is, every mountain starts in a valley. Everyone wants to stand on the mountaintops and be successful, confident, steady, blessed and strong, but no one starts there at first; because to reach the peak, you must begin low.

You must climb, you must walk step by step and you must trust that the God who called you upward will strengthen you to keep going. We also forget that you cannot leap from mountain to mountain, that you must come down into the valley before climbing to the next peak. The valley does not mean failure, it means change. It is where God restores breath, strengthens legs, renews vision and redirects the path for our next climb.

So today, if you are on the mountain, know that your view is a testimony of God's faithfulness, so stay humble, stay grateful and stay surrendered to Him. If you are in the valley, remember this as well, you are not buried you are only being prepared for the next mountain.

Never forget that the same God of the mountain is the God of the valley and the God of every tunnel in between.

Wherever you are today whether in the tunnel, valley, or mountaintop, just invite God into your journey. Look for Him in the dark places, trust Him in the low places and praise Him in the high places. Your path has purpose, your steps are ordered, and your story is not finished. Keep going. God is leading you through every passage and up every mountain.

Reflection

Which season are you currently in, is it the tunnel, valley, or the mountain? How is God inviting me to trust Him there?

What is one step of faith you can take this week to move forward, even if the path feels unclear?

Prayer

Lord, thank You for being with me in every season. Guide me through the tunnels, strengthen me in the valleys, and humble me on the mountains. Help me trust Your hand even when I cannot see Your plan. Lead me, sustain me, and draw me closer to You each day. In Jesus name Amen.

Chapter 73

When the Sparrows Came

Matthew 10:29–31 (NIV)
"Are not two sparrows sold for a penny? Yet not one of them will fall to the ground outside your Father's care. And even the very hairs of your head are all numbered. So don't be afraid; you are worth more than many sparrows."

Sometimes God uses the smallest wings to deliver the biggest messages.

I had moved to a new city only a few months earlier when something began to shift in my awareness. It started the day a sparrow stopped by my window for a simple moment, but that moment stirred something in me. From that day on, I began to pay closer attention when I encountered birds and even made it a habit to pass by my car at least once a day, where it sat parked beneath a tree by the roadside, so I could see the birds.

One particular day stood out, as I approached my vehicle, I noticed two sparrows circling around it dipping low, darting in and out, almost as if they were playing hide and seek. There were many other cars parked beneath the same tree, yet the "game" was happening only around mine.

The closer I got, the more curious I became and I expected them to fly away as soon as I got near to them, but they did not. They continued dancing around the car even as I stood just inches away, and only when I reached out my hand did they finally fly away.

Later, when I shared the experience with a friend, he told me something that confirmed in my spirit; birds especially sparrows, are often seen as messengers. Just like the birds Noah sent out in Genesis, they can appear as divine reminders, signs of comfort, or carriers of subtle messages. "They are not afraid of the one who is meant to receive the message," he said.

That thought stayed with me and from that day to this one, my discernment deepened. I now pay attention to what many people would dismiss as "ordinary" moments things that seem small, simple, unimportant. I now know that sometimes the most extraordinary messages from God arrive wrapped in ordinary moments.

Sparrows remind us that God often speaks in whispers, not shouts, in gentle signs, not loud statements and in subtle movements, not in a dramatic fashion. If we are not paying attention, we might miss the message that He sent right to our doorstep.

So promise yourself today to slow down, look more closely and allow your spirit to be present enough to receive the quiet messages God sends your way. The smallest moments carry big meaning when your eyes and heart are open. Ask God to help you notice the divine in the everyday as He is speaking sometimes through tiny wings hovering right beside you.

Reflection

Have you ever experienced something small a moment in nature, a gesture, a coincidence that felt like more than just chance?

What might God be saying through things you didn't understand in the moment, but now look back on with fresh eyes?

Prayer

Father, thank You for the quiet ways You speak. Sometimes even through the birds, through beauty and through timing that doesn't make sense until much later.
Help me slow down enough to notice your presence. To remember what I once rushed past and to believe that even when I feel unseen, you are sending signs of love. In Jesus name Amen.

Chapter 74

The Exit Ramp

Proverbs 3:5-6 (NIV)
"Trust in the Lord with all your heart and lean not on your own understanding; in all your ways submit to him, and he will make your paths straight".

Assumptions create passengers in our minds, but purpose reveals who truly meant to ride with us because not everyone in your lane is going your way.

For over a year, every Sunday I would take a forty-five-minute drive along the highway to church. It is not my favorite stretch of road because the traffic moves too fast, the drivers too hasty and the journey too quiet for my liking. Yet I had grown used to the rhythm of it, the roar of tires, the blur of signs and the long stretches of open lanes.

What I had come to realize is that I make a lot of assumptions on that highway. I often glance around at the cars beside me and imagine we were all going the same way, heading to the same destination. It is always a comforting thought sometimes; until one by one, they take their exit. Always to the right and off they go, and suddenly I am alone again.

At first it used to disturb me and I would feel a sense of loss, even though I did not know one of them. Then one Sunday as the last car beside me swerved off unexpectedly, I heard a whisper in my spirit: "Stop assuming they are meant to go all the way with you."

I gripped the steering wheel tighter and thought that it was not just about the highway, it was about life. So many times, we assume that certain people are meant to journey with us forever. We think of sharing direction, sharing vision and sometimes even sharing purpose; until they take an exit we did not expect, and we are left alone, hurt and confused.

It can even tempt us to question our own route, but what if the path you are on is designed to be a little lonelier because it is a little holier?

God never promised we would always have company in our calling. He promised His presence and not always the approval of others. The highway to purpose is sometimes wide open and quiet, with few traveling beside you, but that does not mean you are lost; it just means you are following your own divine route.

Nowadays each time I see someone exit from a road or highway I try to say a silent prayer for them. I thank God I am still moving forward, still being led and still being developed even when the road is empty. I am not alone; I am just in alignment with my assignment.

Reflection

Remember this: Not everyone in your lane is going your way, so in what area of your life have you built up assumptions about others?

Make your own notes as to how this story has impacted your life and maybe you recall one of your own. Pray that God will give you faith to trust him more.

Prayer

Dear God, I have harbored beliefs all my life about different things, even some that does not really matter. Help me to release myself from assumptions and to trust that you will lead and direct me.

Chapter 75

The Quiet Strength of Faith

Part 1: The Selfless Faith of a Mother

Psalm 34:18 (NIV)
"The Lord is close to the brokenhearted and saves those who are crushed in spirit."

The heart that gives without counting the cost, the hand that serves without seeking to be recognized these are the marks of a love that reflects God's own heart.

There are moments in life when we meet souls whose quiet acts of love radiate more brightly than any sermon. My mother was such a soul, she did not serve to be seen but she served because she believed God saw it all. Her life overflowed with a generosity that defied reason, giving away the last portion of food, sharing the little we had, placing herself in the background so others could move to the front.

She did this not because she had much but because she trusted the God who multiplies the little. Mama lived every day as though His provision was secured because when we lacked anything her words never changed, it is always "God will provide."

Her life reminds us that faith is not sure when everything is easy, but when everything is scarce and yet we choose to trust God anyway.

You may be in a season now like my mother was, giving your best, pouring out what feels like your last drop, trusting God even when you cannot see the outcome.

If so, let her example remind you that God sees the sacrifices no one else sees. God honors the faith no one else applauds. Continue to serve with a willing heart, for your quiet obedience is shaping a testimony far greater than you know.

Reflection

Think carefully, what areas of your life do you struggle to trust God with and how can you grow a faith that is unshaken by circumstances?

How can you serve others in a way that reflects God's heart of selfless love and trust in His provision?

Prayer

Lord, thank You for the example of those who live their lives with a quiet, unwavering faith. May we follow in their footsteps, trusting You even when the road is hard, serving others without expecting anything in return, and living in the assurance that You know all things best. We ask that You strengthen our faith, give us hearts of compassion, and remind us that You are near to the brokenhearted. In Jesus' name, In Jesus name Amen.

Chapter 76

The Enduring Power of a Faithful Life

Part 2: The Quiet Strength of Faith

Even when you cannot see the purpose, cling to the truth that God love never leaves you, even when you are in the valley.

The day my mother suffered a stroke, life changed instantly. Her body was not the same, neither was her mind. Her speech faded and after a while suffering became her constant companion. Yet her faith remained untouched.

She never complained, never murmured, never questioned God. Though at times she did not know the words she said, we never heard her questioning God. After months of silence her final words broke through like a divine whisper: "God knows all things best."

Those words carry a depth only those who have suffered can truly understand to the point where we had to engrave those words on her tombstone, "God knows all things best".

Today those words, God knows all things best, are the same as the day we buried her in April of year 2000. Her life teaches us that faith does not collapse in hardship it only deepens, and that God's presence in suffering is not always loud, but always near.

You may be in a season like I was, watching someone you love suffer, praying prayers that feel heavy, asking God for mercy. Or perhaps you are facing a trial that shakes your soul. If so, take hear because God is near, God is working and don't forget that God still knows all things best. Even when you cannot see the purpose, cling to the truth that His love never leaves you even when you are in the lowest valley.

Reflection

What areas of your life do you struggle to trust God with, and how can you practice a deeper surrender?

How can you begin serving others in small, selfless ways that reflect God's heart and your own growing faith?

Prayer

Lord, thank You for the powerful testimonies of those who demonstrate quiet, steadfast faith. Help me to trust You in seasons of scarcity, suffering, or uncertainty. Teach me to give generously, love deeply, and follow You with unwavering confidence. Strengthen my heart to believe that You truly know all things best. In Jesus' name, In Jesus name Amen.

www.ingramcontent.com/pod-product-compliance
Lightning Source LLC
LaVergne TN
LVHW090601110826
845146LV00001B/221

* 9 7 9 8 9 9 4 3 3 3 5 0 1 *